酒
SAKE

FIRST PUBLISHED IN 2015 BY NEW HOLLAND PUBLISHERS PTY LTD
LONDON • SYDNEY • AUCKLAND

THE CHANDLERY, UNIT 9, 50 WESTMINSTER BRIDGE ROAD, LONDON SE1 7QY, UNITED KINGDOM
1/66 GIBBES STREET, CHATSWOOD, NSW 2067, AUSTRALIA
5/39 WOODSIDE AVENUE, NORTHCOTE, AUCKLAND 0627, NEW ZEALAND

WWW.NEWHOLLANDPUBLISHERS.COM

A RECORD OF THIS BOOK IS HELD AT THE BRITISH LIBRARY AND THE NATIONAL LIBRARY OF AUSTRALIA.

ISBN: 978 1 74257 561 2

MANAGING DIRECTOR: FIONA SCHULTZ
PROJECT EDITOR: HOLLY WILLSHER
DESIGNER: THOMAS CASEY
PRODUCTION DIRECTOR: OLGA DEMENTIEV
PRINTER: TOPPAN LEEFUNG PRINTING LIMITED

10 9 8 7 6 5 4 3 2 1

KEEP UP WITH NEW HOLLAND PUBLISHERS ON FACEBOOK
WWW.FACEBOOK.COM/NEWHOLLANDPUBLISHERS

酒
SAKE

Hideo Dekura

NEW HOLLAND

CONTENTS

Welcome to the Art of Sake 7
Introduction 8
Sake 10
Shochu 25
List of Sake Brewers 30

=\|=\|=\|=\|=\|=\|=\|=\|=\|=\|=\|=\|=\|=\|=\|=\|=

SAKE BREWERS/BRANDS

Bungo Meijyo 34
Bunraku 36
Chiyomusubi 38
Daishichi 40
Ginban 44
Godo Shusei 45
Hakushika 46
Hakutsuru 48
Harushika 50
Ichinokura 54
Ippongi 58
Kagura 62
Kidoizumi 64
Kitanohomare 66

Kobe Shu-shin-kan 68
Mikunihare 70
Miyazaki Honten 72
Nakajimaya 74
Otokoyama 76
Satsuma 80
Sekihara 82
Sudohonke 84
Taiwakura 86
Tamanohikari 88
Taruhei 92
Tsukasabotan 94
Urakasumi 99
Yoshikubo 102

=\|=\|=\|=\|=\|=\|=\|=\|=\|=\|=\|=\|=\|=\|=\|=\|=

RECIPES

Basics 106
Otsumami (nibbling) 114
Vegetables 126
Sushi and Sashimi 152
Fish 170
Meat and Poultry 214

=\|=\|=\|=\|=\|=\|=\|=\|=\|=\|=\|=\|=\|=\|=\|=\|=

Acknowledgements 232

WELCOME TO THE ART OF SAKE

Mr Hideo Dekura is the author of many books on Japanese cuisine, his new book *Sake* 酒 will delight lovers of good food and wine.

Nothing beats a good sake. This wonderful drink is built on two simple things – rice and water –transformed by many centuries of traditional skills and knowledge. Sake is culture in Japan and sake making is an art form.

There is a great variety of sake to enjoy, and this book introduces sake from many regions of Japan. It contains some of my favourite sake brands and others I have yet to explore. I am looking forward to doing so soon – matching them with a couple of *Sake*'s appetizing recipes.

Sake is an integral part of Japanese cuisine. Sake loves food, and food loves sake. After you read *Sake*, I am sure you will want to try the sake and recipes for yourself. Simply browsing through *Sake* will make your mouth water; the beautiful photography excites the senses.

This very attractive and informative book will be an excellent reference and a joy to read. I hope you accept its invitation and explore the world of sake with Hideo Dekura as your expert guide.

Cheers, or 乾杯！ (Kampai!) as we say in Japan.

Masato Takaoka
Consul-General of Japan, Sydney

INTRODUCTION

Let me begin by introducing myself and why I am very excited to be involved with this book. My name is Hideo Dekura. I have been a chef and food writer for over half a century. During that time I have published quite a number of books, I have also specialised in traditional Japanese cooking, modern classic Japanese and French classic cuisine. I was born in Yotsuya, which makes up part of the central area of Tokyo.

My culinary education began with me spending my childhood in two Japanese restaurants both owned by my family. The restaurants specialised in the preparation of traditional Japanese food. Those restaurants, Kihei and Misuji were handed down from generation to generation in my family.

Hospitality has been a passion since my earliest days, which were spent watching my grandfather, father and then my brother supplying premium food to the many regulars who frequented those restaurants. Now, in my senior years, I find myself in the fortunate position to have the chance to explain how the sublime marriage of sake and Japanese food has developed over the centuries. Sake and the food it accompanies still presents me with many questions that need to be answered. It is not yet an exact science even for me or many of my countrymen. Therefore I can only imagine how difficult it must be for people who have not been exposed to the complexities that that marriage shares. Is it simply the flavour, tradition, it's interaction with traditional and contemporary Japanese food or a combination of all three? That is the often re-occurring question I have kept asking myself during my many years of enjoying sake. I assure you it will become a question that all new enthusiasts will ask themselves as they begin their own journey. One thing is for sure, that sake is a drink that can be enjoyed on all occasions.

Some people enjoy happy times with a friend or partner, while many seem to be happy with their own company. Others might find solace when they find themselves in a lonely situation. Couples can create beautifully romantic and intimate moments

for each other. Festivals, birthdays, a promotion at work, or the birth of a new addition to the family, even the finishing of a new home, sake is often the common theme all those moments share. One thing my life has taught me is that it is a very magical drink indeed. It is now up to a new generation to take the reins and find contemporary ways to enjoy sake and to help guide it by taking its rightful place as a world drink. Like a good wine or beer, sake is now enjoyed with a variety of cuisines. It is not a pleasure that should be limited to only the Japanese.

This book, my latest, has been designed to introduce information and explanations about matching different sakes and cuisines. As part of this introduction to the enjoyment of sake, I will begin by highlighting 28 of the most respected Kuramotos (sake brewers) in Japan. Each of the 28 brewers will be individually explained; their methods and what gives each product its individual characteristics. You will become aware of the strong work ethic needed in achieving the respected and admired level of each Kuramoto's workmanship. This book is intended as a beginners guide to sake. I am sure some readers will go on a journey of self-discovery into the more intensive details of various makers of the very coolest Japanese sake brands.

I would really like, just at the beginning, for you to enjoy the simpler journey of exploring sake and Japanese cuisine.

SAKE 酒

Sake and its significant and long lasting relationship with Japanese cuisine.

History and background

Once sake used to have distinctive categories. Tokkyu (premium grade), Ikkyu (first grade), etc. Now there have been new categories added, those changes have developed into names including 'Junmai-ginjyo', 'Dai-ginjyo', 'Honjyozoshu', etc. Now, even more contemporary styles have been introduced which include types of sake called 'Happo-shu' (sparkling sake).

Traditionally, sake rice was sourced from the local growers. It must be remembered that sake rice and cooking rice are not the same product. Sake rice is a specific grain used solely for the making of sake. Different grades of grain produce different flavours, varying so much that now, some sake brewers (Kuramotos) produce their own individual sake rice for use only in their production line. This is a fascinating development in the production of this intrinsically Japanese product, similar to the right choice of grape for a certain style of wine or a particular grain or fruit in the making of spirits. The sourcing of the individual rice and its particular flavour closely aligns with the new trend of matching fusion cuisine with its individual sake. Again, similar to certain wine varieties being better suited to types of food. Through the years sake has been thought of as Japan's national drink. However, it has now reached popularity on a global level and the number of fans is continually growing around world. At present, the understanding of sake, and how to enjoy it, in the western world, is completely different from wine. In the West, sake is often treated as nothing more than a trendy drink. Even groups of the supposed 'Intellectual Sake Society' hold discussions about how to enjoy drinking sake. For example, what sort of sake cup is used at a special occasion? Should the eldest be given the sake first? Is the sake better cold or warm? Is it only for ceremonial use or for pleasure? These customs are already known and practised by Japanese. In Japan sake is just a part of life. I feel that a majority of foreign sake lovers are taking sake in a new direction, which is far different to the traditional sake culture of Japan.

When I think back over the 70 years of Japanese life I have enjoyed, the way that sake is now promoted onto the world stage is greatly different to when I was first stepping out into the restaurant world. Japanese producers used to export sake to the USA and other countries with an assumption that it would be consumed in accordance with Japan's traditional manner, which, in those times would have been considered as 'fairly conservative'. Now, thanks to that export market, sake drinking has taken on a whole new world of opportunities. Even the Japanese are enjoying a new wave of sake society.

In the Nara-cho era in Japan (710–794). One particular book, called 'Fuudoki' (natural future) wrote about the primitive ways involved in the fermentation process used to produce sake. The sake fermentation process was thought of as a gift from god. Even in 'Ko-dai' (ancient times) how to make sake was recorded, by an unknown person, it was written that to begin, first chew grains of rice in the mouth, when crushed into a paste place into an urn to begin the fermentation process stage. Therefore, the Japanese believe sake was a sophisticated message given to the people so they could enjoy the tastes and sensations that sake offers. That once basic method of production has now grown into the unique process which is pushing itself into what can be considered a truly modern global era of enjoyment.

Sake has definitely attracted new admirers from around the globe. It can no longer be considered as a drink limited to the palettes of the Japanese. Sake is destined to take on legendary status as a world drink. For those who are newcomers to this liquid delight, be prepared to take-off into the infinite delights of great pleasure this sake journey will give to you in the future. As with any alcoholic drink, treat sake with respect and it will become a wonderful companion.

Currently in Japan there are over 5000 varieties of sake. These are being produced by over 1300 different brewers. Sake is deeply involved and related to Honzen-ryori (main stream Japanese classic cuisine), Kaiseki-ryori (Base of banquet Japanese cuisine), Chakai-seki (Tea ceremony cuisine), which are all different forms of traditional Japanese cuisine involving sake. Sake is also a great companion to home cooking, which is called 'ban-shaku' (enjoying sake at every dinner at home). Home cooking used to be the preparation of only Japanese style of dishes. However, the Japanese home kitchen has now adopted food styles from around the world as standard fare. The Japanese palette is enjoying a huge variety of cuisines to mix with sake in the home environment. This world-wide acceptance of sake has in fact had a two pronged effect of sharing sake and food from around the world.

To help achieve the great pleasure sake will impart to you and your friends, I will now share some technical hints I have gained over the years for combining sake and great food.

1 Typically, there are three different ways that sake is presented for drinking. Okan (heated warm sake), Reishu (chilled sake), Hiya (room temperature but poured on ice when served).

2 Sake is traditionally served in an Ochoko made from ceramic or porcelain. Currently cups made of glass, ceramic and porcelain, or even western wine glasses are used.

As with fine wines the type and shape of the chosen container will greatly vary the flavour and complexities your particular sake will have.

1 Some cups, which have wider and more open top edges, will allow the aroma of the sake to be enjoyed more clearly.

2 Other cups can be used to express seasonable atmosphere or will be used for special occasions.

Japan, through the centuries, has developed individual regional cuisines that have accompanying sake styles. Brewers have created such distinctive flavours and characteristics within their product that their sakes are often considered as masterpieces of the Brewer's trade. Nowadays, many sake lovers, as with wine lovers, consider that the best product often attracts the highest price. Good sake along with the best sake will achieve a market value which is dictated by demand.

How to make delicious warm or hot sake
Text ©Hakutsuru

There are various ways to make warm or hot sake, but the best way is in hot water. It has been said that the number one way to enjoy warm or hot sake is to put sake into a sake jar ('tokkuri'), place the sake jar into a pot of hot water (of about 98°C (208°F)) and then to heat the sake to the desired temperature (never boil sake). The standard is to look into the sake vessel and if there are small bubbles swelling up, then the sake is considered warm (about 40°C (104°F)), or if the bubbles immediately rise to the surface, then the sake is considered hot (50°C (122°F)). The standard time for leaving the sake vessel in the hot water is about 2 to 2.5 minutes for 180ml (6fl oz) ('ichigo'). The sake is poured into a small sake cup ('ochoko') or a larger sized cup ('guinomi') and consumed.

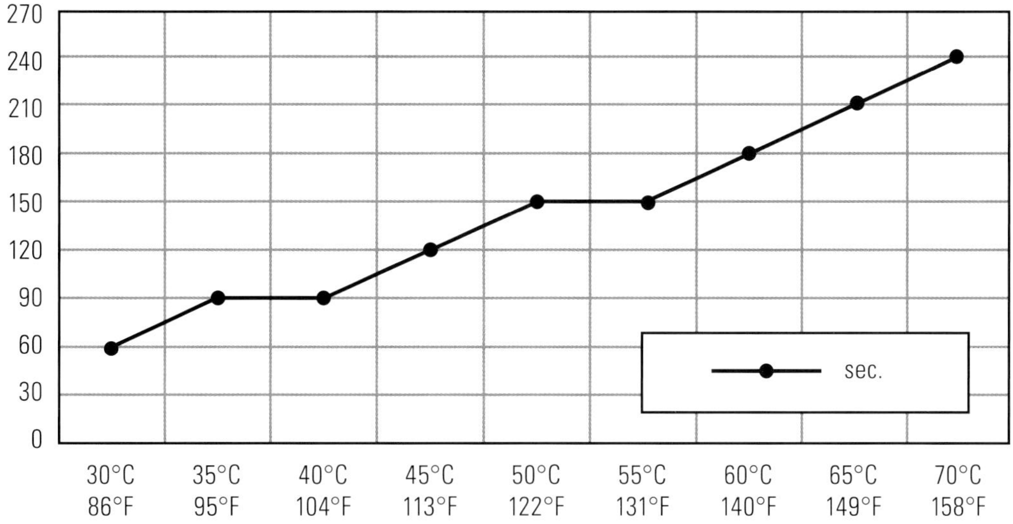
270
240
210
180
150
120
90
60
30
0
sec.
30°C 86°F
35°C 95°F
40°C 104°F
45°C 113°F
50°C 122°F
55°C 131°F
60°C 140°F
65°C 149°F
70°C 158°F

Time standard for delicious warm or hot sake (when the heated sake is made with boiled water of about 98°C (208°F)

Enjoying Chilled sake

The temperature at which to drink cold sake is about 8°C (46°F). In the middle of summer, however, some people prefer to drink sake below 5°C (41°F). When the temperature is high, cold products are felt to be delicious, and in this light, the subtle aroma of Japanese sake gives a richness to the taste. In particular, because the smell of fresh sake and a sharp taste are characteristic of delicious draft sake, it harmonizes wonderfully when adjusting to light sweet and sour foods. In addition, cold sake will even wash away the lingering aftertaste of oily foods.

We recommend sake be consumed in a small way, i.e., in mouthful units, such as with a small elegant glass, wine glass or crystal.

joukan	hot sake (around 50°C (122°F))
nurukan	Warm sake (around 40°C (104°F))
hitohadakan	lukewarm sake (around 35°C (95°F))
jouon	sake served at room temperature
reishu	chilled sake (5°C (41°F) to around 8°C (46°F))
kanzake	hot or warm sake

End text ©Hakutsuru

How to drink responsibly with sake

1 As with the consumption of any alcoholic beverage, it should be doneresponsibly.

2 Select 'Junmai-shu' or sake of good quality.

3 Sit back, relax and enjoy the flavour of sake.

4 Remember … quality not quantity.

Although the technical expertise of the Toji (master of sake) can never be dismissed. I look forward with great anticipation, to the sophisticated ideas and advice from a newer and modern generation of sake brewer. Marketing teams are becoming very aware that the right product needs to be placed strategically to maximise its customer potential.

How to match sake with food?

1 Within sake the aroma and the intrinsic flavour of the food combines perfectly to produce a natural synergy.

2 There is a symbiotic effect with sake. Sake enhances the taste of food and food enhances the taste of sake.

3 Sake is a natural palette cleanser.

4 Sake will naturally lighten the taste of rich foods.

5 Sake helps prevent odours from strongly scented foods, such as some fish or meats. At the same time, it actually helps to enhance the hidden flavours that are often masked by those stronger tastes. Surprisingly sake interacts well with dairy products such as cheese and cream. For example, if you want to achieve a smoother taste or aroma of food you should try sake as a liquid to thin the sauces of other cuisines. After some first possibly timid attempts your journey of combining sake into your day to day cooking adventures will have begun. You will be surprised and inspired by the new taste and Umami that is imparted into your food.

I would also like to mention my 7 point check list for the taste evaluation of sake.

1   Your first interaction with sake will be through your sense of smell. That first hint of aroma will prepare your body for the taste that will shortly be enjoyed.

2   You should, and will, taste with your tongue. The attack of flavour will instantly happen on your palette.

3   It is during that initial contact that the acidity and sweetness will be determined.

4   The taste evaluation of all the elements acidity, sweetness and umami will quickly be determined.

5   However, your senses will gradually describe and grade the characteristic values in greater detail.

6   It is essential that the combined sensation of flavour by nose and tongue should be pleasant.

7   After the sake is swallowed, is when you should pick up the remaining flavours and individuality from the sake you have chosen.

Sake for cooking

The next part of the sake journey involves my first passion, food and the combining of my ever-developing exploration of the possibilities that the intricacies of sake offers.

Here are some examples:

1   Sake is an amino acid. Meaning that the alcohol will enhance the flavour of food during the cooking process.

2   Sake is considered to have umami (the 5th taste sensation) a full bodied and rich taste.

3   Sake's fermentation process helps to bring a natural balance of flavours. After fermentation the by-products, which are referred to as Kome-koji, (rice malt) and Sake-kasu (sake lee/rice pulp) can be used for cooking.

4   In grilled, steamed or boiled dishes.

5   Sake can also be used as a final adjustment when cooking. Similar to adding a splash of wine at the end of the cooking process with many western dishes.

Many consider sake less sour than wine, which is why sake is often considered to be more easily matched with certain foods. The future of sake has unlimited opportunities to be incorporated into the ongoing gastronomical challenge that contemporary chefs continually face.

Advanced sake making process

1 Brown rice

2 Rice polishing

3 White rice

4 Washing with water

4 Steeping

5 Steaming

6 Steamed rice

7 Cooling

8 Starter mash (with Rice kouji and water. Yeast)

9 Main mash (stage 1. 2. 3.)

10 Fermentation

11 Pressing (comes out sake lees)

12 Sake. Raw and undiluted

Note: between the processes of fermentation to pressing, alcohol additives can be permitted.

Cf: Chart for processing sake brewing (opposite) by Urakasumi

©Urakasumi Saura Co., Ltd

Making sake at Urakasumi

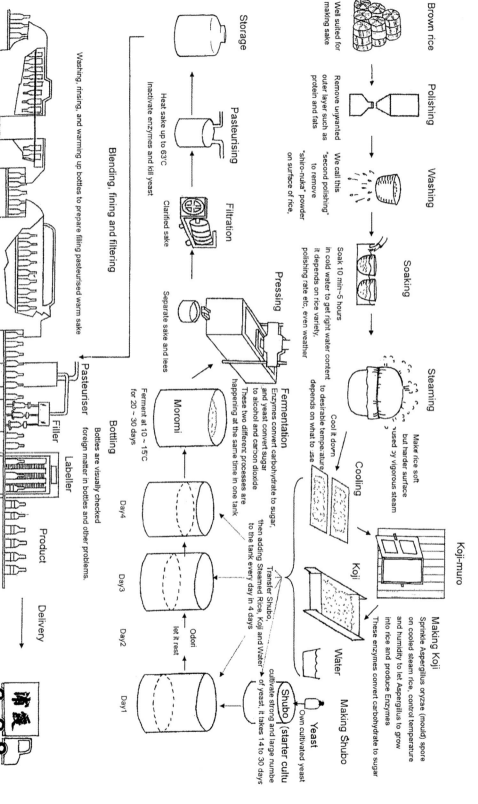

Brown rice — Well suited for making sake

Polishing — Remove unwanted outer layer such as protein and fats

Washing — We call this "second polishing" to remove "shiro-nuka" powder on surface of rice.

Soaking — Soak 10 min~5 hours in cold water to get right water content, it depends on rice variety, polishing rate etc, even weather

Steaming — Make rice soft but harder surface, used by vigorous steam

Cooling — Cool it down to desirable temperature, depends on what to use

Koji-muro / **Koji**

Making Koji — Sprinkle Aspergillus oryzae (mould) spore on cooled steam rice, control temperature and humidity to let Aspergillus to grow into rice and produce Enzymes. These enzymes convert carbohydrate to sugar

Water

Making Shubo — **Shubo** (starter cultu... cultivate strong and large numbe of yeast, it takes 14 to 30 days

Yeast — Own cultivated yeast

Fermentation — Enzymes convert carbohydrate to sugar, and yeast convert sugar to alcohol and carbon dioxide. These two different processes are happening at the same time in one tank

Transfer Shubo, then adding Steamed Rice, Koji and Water to the tank every day in 4 days

Moromi — Ferment at 10 ~ 15°C for 20 ~ 30 days

Day1 — Odori / let it rest / Day2 / Day3 / Day4

Pressing — Separate sake and lees

Filtration — Clarified sake

Pasteurising — Inactivate enzymes and kill yeast. Heat sake up to 63°C

Storage

Blending, fining and filtering

Pasteuriser — Washing, rinsing, and warming up bottles to prepare filling pasteurised warm sake

Filler

Bottling — Bottles are visually checked foreign matter in bottles and other problems.

Labeller

Product

Delivery

Ingredients

To produce sake, rice and water are the most crucial ingredients for the sake brewers. Shuzuo Kotekimai or sake rice are the types of rice which are suitable for brewing sake.

Water

Water is one of the important elements for producing sake. It is used for rinsing, soaking, processing the steamed rice, and diluting the sake.

The water called 'shikomi mizu', is specially prepared water designed solely to be used in the production of sake. Each Shuzo (sake brewer) carefully choose a shikomi mizu that best delivers the flavours they want to imply. This choice of water is what the Shuzo uses to emphasize their individual character.

Hard water is considered ideal. It contains suitable minerals, such as magnesium (Mg) and potassium (K) to help the fermentation process. But water that contains an excess of metallic elements, such as iron, manganese (Mn) or copper (Cu) is not suitable for sake as it creates unwanted acidity and discolouring.

Sakamai 酒米(sake rice) or Shuzo-kotekimai 酒造好適米 (best sake rice) Types of rice suitable to brew sake

Ordinarily the size of the sake rice grain is bigger than the common short grain rice used for cooking, as the Shinpaku, (core of a rice grain), is considered to produce excellent sake a larger grain means a larger core is left over after polishing. Since the size of the sake rice is larger it is also heavier which makes it more delicate to harvest during the typhoon season.

Ideal Sakamai has a greater content of starch and less protein, it also absorbs water easier which in turn is smoother to convert into sugar.

Here are the most popular brand of sake rice:

- Yamada-nishiki 山田錦: Originated and registered in Hyogo prefecture in 1936.

- Gohyaku-mangoku 五百万石: Originated and registered in Niigata prefecture in 1957.

- Miyama nishiki 美山錦: Originated in Nagano in 1972 but not registered until 1978.

- Omachi 雄町: One of the oldest sake rice varieties. The earliest recorded harvest was around 1866, then it was called Nihongusa. It was registered as Omachi in 1924.

Seimai-buai 精米歩合

Seimai is the first important process in producing sake. Carefully polishing off the outer layer of grain which contains protein and fat, to reduce the unpleasant taste.

Seimai-buai is a ratio described in percentages. If Seimai-buai is 70%, it means 70% of polished rice, in other words 70 kg of polished rice derived from 100 kg of brown rice. The lower the percentage, the higher the quality will be.

Less polished sake rice generally contains a stronger and miscellaneous taste, on the other hand a greater polishing ratio, (a lower percentage), gives a clear fragrant flavour.

Categories Sake 1
Classification by the Japanese National Tax Agency

Futsu-shu 普通酒 is a general term for drinking sake, 'futsu' means normal or standard. It is used on sake which does not constrict to any particular regulations of Seimai-buai, sake koji or rice.

Tokutei-meisho sake 特定名称酒

However there are three specified types which are classified by the national Tax Agency. They are Ginjyo-shu (吟醸酒), Junmai-shu 純米酒、Honjozo-shu 本醸造酒. These sake are called Tokutei-meisho (特定名称酒) sake and they must all use more than 15% of Kome-koji.

Ginjo-shu, 吟醸酒 uses sake rice polished up-to 60% of seimai-buai sake rice. Brewed using the Ginjo-zukuri process, this is the process of a low temperature fermentation. It creates a characteristic flavour called, Ginjyo-ko which has a splendid aroma. Dai Ginjo-shu 大吟醸酒 is a type of Ginjo-shu but uses sake rice polished up to 50 %. Junmai-ginjo-shu 純米吟醸酒 is Ginjo-shu but does not use distilled alcohol. Junmai-Dai-ginjo shu 純米大吟醸酒 is Ginjo-shu that uses sake rice polished up to 50% and does not use distilled alcohol, made from rice and kome-koji.

Junmai-shu, 純米酒 is only made from rice and kome-koji (malted koji rice), without using distilled alcohol and does not conform to Seimai-buai regulations. However, Tokubetsu-Junmai-shu 特別純米酒 (Special Junmai-shu) uses polished sake rice (around 60% seimai-buai).

Honjozo-shu本醸造酒 uses sake rice polished up-to 70%. Tokubetu Honjozo-shu 特別本醸造酒 uses sake rice polished below 60%.

The 8 names they are categorised into can be found on the label of the bottles. Below they are listed phonetically.

- Jun-mai-shu   純米酒
- Toku-betu-jun-mai-shu   特別純米酒
- Jin-mai-gin-jo-shu   純米吟醸酒
- Jin-mai-dai-gin-jo shu   純米大吟醸酒
- Gin-jo-shu   吟醸酒
- Dai-gin-jo-shu   大吟醸酒
- Hon-jo-zo-shu   本醸造酒
- Toku-betsu-hon-jo-zo-shu   特別本醸造酒

Opposite text ©Tatsuuma-Honke Brewing Co.,Ltd.

Premium Sake Classes

The Japanese National Tax Agency officially recognizes 8 premium 'Special Designated Sake Types' (*Tokutei Meisho no Seishu*) based on very strict standards. These varieties vary according to minimum rice polishing ratio and whether a small amount of brewer's alcohol has been added in the fermentation process.

Special Designation	Ingredients	Minimum Rice Polishing Ratio	Brewer's Alcohol
Junmai	Water, Rice, Koji Rice	No specification	None
Honjozo	Water, Rice, Koji Rice, Brewer's Alcohol	70%	Volume must be less than 10% of content of polished rice
Tokubetsu Honjozo	Water, Rice, Koji Rice, Brewer's Alcohol	60% or Special Brewing Process	Volume must be less than 10% of content of polished rice
Tokubetsu Junmai	Water, Rice, Koji Rice	60% or Special Brewing Process	None
Ginjo	Water, Rice, Koji Rice, Brewer's Alcohol	60%	Volume must be less than 10% of content of polished rice
Ginjo Junmai	Water, Rice, Koji Rice,	60%	None
Daiginjo	Water, Rice, Koji Rice, Brewer's Alcohol	50%	Volume must be less than 10% of content of polished rice
Daiginjo Junmai	Water, Rice, Koji Rice	50%	None

Categories of Sake 2
According to the process

Genshu 原酒 Undiluted sake
Sake is diluted with water before bottling. This brings down the alcohol volume and flavour. Genshu, being undiluted, has a higher percentage and a more robust palate.

Nama-zake 生酒 Unpasteurized 'live' sake
Although yeast and koji mold are intrinsic parts of the sake making process, these microorganisms need to be pasteurized (heat treated) before storage and repeated before shipping. Due to the advances in refrigerated storage, it has been made possible to produce unpasteurized sake. This Nama-zake has a rougher taste commonly known in Japan as 'Koji-bana' 麹花. As the microorganisms are still live, Nama-zake will not last well without refrigeration and once opened alcohol should be consumed as soon as possible.

Categories of Sake 3
According to its characters

Ori-zake and Nigori-zake 濁り酒 Cloudy sake
There are two types of white sake, Ori-zake and Nigori-zake. Although visually very similar the process in which they are made is very different.

Ori-zake
Sake is returned to a tank for final filtration before storage. After several days a fine sediment, (lees), collects at the base. This is discarded, and the clear sake is stored. Ori-zake is stored and packaged without removing this sediment, giving it a milky slightly thicker texture and flavour.

Nigori-zake 濁り酒 Cloudy sake
Nigori-zake's process is during the pressing stage. After sake is fermented it is pressed to separate the undissolved rice from the sake, Nigori-zake leaves this inside and the result is a sweeter rawer sake. It's colour ranges from translucent to a solid white, and the texture from slightly dense to quite thick where a utensil is almost needed to consume.

Taru-zake 樽酒 sake brewed in sake barrow

Taru-zake is the only sake that has a strong resemblance to the wine making process. It is stored and aged in Japanese cedar barrels which gives it its distinctive aroma.

At many festivals and celebrations in Japan, sake is served from a wooden barrel and drunk from a 'masu', a Japanese wooden box made from Japanese cypress wood. This 'masu' wasn't always a drinking container but originally was used to measure rice.

Although often confused, the sake presented at celebrations is not true taru-zake, as it is only put into the barrel just before consuming.

Categories of Sake 4
According to traditional sake brewing methods

Yamahai (山廃) and Kimoto (木酛) are two traditional variations of the brewing method, where the yeast starter is made in a way that allows more funky yeast and bacteria to be present. The result is a deeper gamier flavour.

Yamahai-zukuri 山廃 Yamahai Method

Originally poles were rammed into the vat for hours to mix and crush the rice and koji into a smooth paste. It was believed this had to be done to properly convert the starches to sugars. This process was called 'Yama-oroshi'. In 1909 it was discovered that this was unnecessary, as the enzymes in the koji would dissolve the rice. The name Yama-oroshi-haishi, (haishi=to stop), was then shortened to Yamahai.

Kimoto-zukuri 木酛 Kimoto Method

Since the early 1900s, brewers have been introducing a lactic acid when fermenting to cultivate the yeast. It is not added in the Kimoto method and the lactic acid is allowed to develop naturally. Because of this the process takes twice as long as current methods. Due to the wilder overtones in both Kimoto and Yamahai-zake, they are more commonly used for Junmai-shu grade sake, but have also been used to successfully produce Ginjo and Daiginjo sake.

Categories of Sake 5

Happo-shu 発泡酒 Sparkling sake
With a lower alcohol level this sparkling sake is often produced with fruity flavours such as lychee, peach and citrus.

Ume-shu 梅酒 Sweet plum sake
Ume-shu is made by shochu or other white liquor and rock sugar accompanied with unripened green ume (Japanese apricot). Because of its sweetness, it is drunk as a dessert liquor or on the rocks.

SHOCHU 焼酎

(Distilled Shonshu Sprit)

Shochu is a Japanese traditional hard liquor, distilled spirits made from grains and vegetables. The most common base ingredients are sweet potato, barley, rice, buckwheat and sugar cane.

'Sake' is a general term for alcohol beverages in Japan. However Nihonshu 日本酒 (Seishu 清酒) is commonly referred to as 'sake' in English speaking countries. Nihonshu and shochu are both traditional Japanese alcoholic beverages, but there are some important differences between them as follows.

Manufacturing Process

Shochu is distilled liquor, similar to brandy and vodka. However Nihonshu is categorized as fermented liquor, putting it in the same category as wine. Grapes are both fermented to make wine and distilled to make brandy. In Japan, rice can be fermented to make Nihonshu, or distilled to make rice shochu. Before Nihonshu became famous in the west, it sometimes used to be referred to as 'rice wine' in acknowledgement of the resemblances between wine making and Nihonshu making.

Alcohol Content

Wine, as a fermented beverage, has a lower alcohol content than distilled liquors. Similarly, Nihonshu, as a fermented beverage, has a lower average alcohol content (13% to 16%) than does shochu. As a distilled beverage, shochu has an average alcohol content of 25% to 37%. Because of its higher alcohol content, shochu can be enjoyed in a variety of ways.

The Main Ingredients

Nihonshu's main ingredient is only rice. Shochu, however, can be made from a number of base ingredients, examples of which include Imo (Japanese sweet potato), barley, rice, buckwheat, and sugar cane. Because each of these base ingredients brings its own unique flavour to the final product, Honkaku Shochu comes in a wide variety of flavours and overtones. This variety in flavour is behind much of the popularity of Honkaku Shochu in Japan.

Serving Style

Nihonshu is usually enjoyed warmed or chilled but shochu is enjoyed in a variety of ways. Because of shochu's higher alcohol content, it can be served straight, on the rocks, mixed with soda or water of different temperatures and also used as a cocktail base.

Additionally, shochu's alcohol level can be changed by adding different amounts of water. So you can enjoy shochu in different ways depending on your body condition, atmosphere and the circumstances around you. Connoisseurs take advantage of the different serving temperatures and styles to accentuate the particular shochu's taste.

For example, in Kagoshima, the home of Imo (sweet potato) Shochu, it is common to enjoy Imo Shochu with hot water at a 60:40 ratio. This serving style enhances the natural sweetness and aroma of the sweet potato (Satsuma Imo). Because shochu matches with wide varieties of foods, it is enjoyed with meals, before meals, and after meals in Japan.

Storage Requirements

Many of the premium Nihonshu need to be kept under refrigeration to maintain its good quality. After the bottle is opened, it is recommended to finish the Nihonshu within about three weeks. Shochu doesn't require this level of care because of its distillation process. As long as shochu is kept in a cool area, away from direct sunlight, the quality will not degrade over time.

Honkaku Shochu　本格焼酎

There are two classifications of shochu in Japan.

The first one is Honkaku Shochu 本格焼酎 (single distillation shochu) and the other is Korui Shochu 甲類焼酎 (consecutive distillation shochu).

They are categorized by Japanese taxation law based on the ingredients and manufacturing method. The word Honkaku is translated as traditional, authentic or genuine.

Honkaku Shochu has restrictions on the ingredients and it has to be made by single distillation, which allows Honkaku Shochu to retain the rich flavour and aroma of its main ingredients.

Kourui Shochu is made by consecutive distillation, which creates a clear taste with no aroma suited for use with cocktail mixers. Their ingredients are varied like molasses, alcohol, and grains. Even though both Honkaku Shochu and Korui Shochu are both called shochu, they have different qualities and characteristics.

History of Shochu

The oldest literature that notes the existence of shochu was written in 1546. Spanish missionary Francisco Xavier sent his adherent Jorge Alvares to Japan before his mission. Jorge stayed in Minami Satsuma (modern day Kagoshima Prefecture) where our company started and wrote a report about Japan. In his post to Xavier, 'Japan Report', he wrote, *'There was Orraqua made from rice.'* 'Orraqua' is a loanword from Arabic that means distilled spirits, and 'Orraqua made from rice' must refer to rice shochu. The oldest extant written record of the Japanese word for shochu was found at Koriyama Hachiman Shrine in Kagoshima prefecture, in graffiti on the roof ridge wood written by a carpenter in 1559. The graffiti said, *'A chief mourner of the shrine was so stingy that he didn't offer me shochu at all'*. This graffiti shows that shochu has been a part of the commoner's life in Kagoshima since the middle of 16th century.

Even though shochu has long been a part of people's life in Satsuma, the shochu of 500 years ago was made from rice and grain. Satsuma Imo didn't exist in Japan at that time. The modern day Kagoshima product, Satsuma Imo Shochu, however, is made from Satsuma Imo (Japanese Sweet Potato). This sweet potato is not native to Japan. Originally it came from Central South America. Then in 1605, it came to Ryukyu Islands (Modern day Okinawa) from Philippines by way of China. About 100 years later, in 1705, it started to spread widely in Kagoshima.

Even though the Satsuma Imo only arrived about 300 years ago, it was so well suited to Kagoshima's climate and environment that it spread extremely quickly. Because it grew so quickly, during a famine in 1732, Satsuma Imo saved many people from starvation and it was so valued.

The people so identified with the newly introduced crop that they began to call it the Satsuma Imo. Even though it is given one name, the Satsuma Imo varies greatly in colour, flavour, and starch content. Because shochu is made from the fermentation of the starch in the base ingredient, the flavours of the final product vary as different base ingredients are used.

Historically, archaeological evidence dates distillation techniques from 3000 BC in Mesopotamia. From Mesopotamia, the technique spread to the western countries like the Arab and eastern countries like India. Distillation techniques were originally used for the production of medicines and perfumes. It was not until the 13th century in China that distillation came to be used for the production of alcoholic beverages. There are three strong theories about the route of the shochu's distillation techniques arrival in Japan.

a) From the China continent coastline, it came to the Northern part of the Island of Kyushu in Japan by way of the Korean peninsula.

b) From the inland of the China continent, by the Silk Road, it came to the northern part of the Island of Kyushu by way of the Korean peninsula.

c) It came from South Asia to the Ryukyu Islands (modern day Okinawa) by the way of Siam (Thailand) then it spread to Amami Oshima Island and went northward in Japan.

Toji Master Brewer's History

In the old days, people were allowed to produce shochu at home without any government permission. But in 1899, the production of shochu came under government regulation by Meiji shogunate. Shochu manufacturers needed to hire professionals and the demand for skilled master brewers called 'Toji' in Japan grew. Here in Kagoshima, the town called Kurose is home to so many of these highly skilled Toji master brewers. At the beginning of the Meiji era, three artisans learned the skill of making shochu with Kuro Koji (Black Koji) from the Ryukyu craftsman. This is the foundation of the modern Imo shochu. After that, they brushed up their skills more and built their own traditions. From generation to generation, the Toji brew masters pass their knowledge only onto those trustworthy who are apprentices to them.

Because of their training and expertise, these Kurose Toji came to be in demand throughout Japan wherever shochu was made. They would go and oversee the seasonal production of shochu in other prefectures, and then return to their hometown of Kurose. Thus Kurose became known as 'the hometown of Toji'.

LIST OF SAKE BREWERS

Note: Sake (酒) is a general-term to describe alcohol drinks in Japanese. But also the word 'sake' is used as 'sake' (rice wine) in English speaking countries. In this book mostly 'sake' is indicated as the latter meaning.

BRAND NAME	COMPANY NAME/WEBSITE	ADDRESS	MAIN PRODUCTS
Bungo Meijyo ぶんご銘醸	ぶんご銘醸　株式会社 Bungo Meijyo Co., Ltd www.bungomeijyo.co.jp	789-4 Naokawa Oaza Yokogawa, Saiki, OITA 879-3105, Japan 大分県佐伯市直川大字横川字亀の甲789番地4	Shochu
Bunraku 文楽	株式会社　文楽 Bunraku Co., Ltd www.bunraku.net	2 Chome-5-5 Kamicho, Ageo, SAITAMA 362-0037, Japan 〒362-0037 埼玉県上尾市上町2丁目5番5号	Sake Shochu
Chiyomusubi 千代むすび	千代むすび酒造株式会社 Chiyomusubi Sake Brewery Co., Ltd www.chiyomusubi.co.jp	131 Taisho-cho, Sakaiminato TOTTORI 684-0004, Japan 鳥取県境港市大正町131	Sake Shochu
Daishichi 大七	大七酒造株式会社 Daishichi Sake Brewery Co., Ltd www.daishichi.com	1-66 Takeda, Nihonmatsu, FUKUSHIMA 964-0902 Japan 福島県二本松市竹田1-66	Sake
Ginban 銀盤	銀盤酒造株式会社 Ginban Shuzo Co., Ltd. www.ginban.co.jp	4853-3 Ogyu, Kurobe, TOYAMA 938-0801, Japan 富山県黒部市荻生4853-3	Sake
Godo Shusei 合同酒精	合同酒精株式会社 Godo Shusei Co., Ltd www.oenon.jp/company/group/godo.html www.oenon.jp/tantakatan/	6-2-10 Ginza, Chuo-ku, TOKYO 104-8162 Japan 東京都中央区銀座6-2-10	Shochu

Hakushika 白鹿	辰馬本家酒造株式会社 Tatsuuma-Honke Brewing Co. Ltd www.hakushika.co.jp	8-21 Kurakakecho, Nishinomiya, HYOGO 662- 0926, Japan 兵庫県西宮市建石町2 番10号	Sake
Hakutsuru 白鶴	白鶴酒造株式会社 Hakutsuru Sake Brewing Co., Ltd www.hakutsuru.co.jp	4-5-5 Sumiyoshi Minamimachi Higashinada Ward, Kobe HYOGO 658- 0041 Japan 兵庫県神戸市東灘区住 吉南町4丁目5-5	Sake Shochu Others
Harushika 春鹿	株式会社 今西清兵衛商店 S. Imanishi Co., Ltd www.harushika.com	4-1 Fukuchi in-cho, Nara- city NARA 630-8381 JAPAN 奈良市福智院町24−1	Sake
Ichinokura 一ノ蔵	株式会社一ノ蔵 Ichinokura Co., Ltd www.ichinokura.co.jp	14 Okeyaki, Matsuyama Sengoku, Osaki city MIYAGI 987-1393 Japan 宮城県大崎市松山千石 字大欅14	Sake
Ippongi 一本義	株式会社一本義久保本店 Ippongi Kubo Honten Co.,Ltd www.ippongi.co.jp	1-3-1 Sawa machı, Katsuyama city FUKUI 911- 8585 Japan 福井県勝山市沢町1丁 目3-1	Sake
Kagura 神楽	神楽酒造株式会社 Kagura Shuzo Co., Ltd www.kagurashuzo.co.jp	144-1 Iwato, Takachiho, Nishiusuki District, MIYAZAKI 882-1621, Japan 宮崎県西臼杵郡高千穂 町岩戸144-1	Shochu
Kidoizumi 木戸泉	木戸泉酒造株式会社 Kidoizumi Shuzo Co., Ltd http://kidoizumi.jpn.com	7635-1 Ohara, Isumi city, CHIBA 298-0004 Japan 千葉県いすみ市大原 7635-1	Sake

Kitanohomare 北の誉	北の誉酒造株式会社 Kitanohomare Shuzo Co., Ltd www.kitanohomare.com	1-21-15 Okusawa, Otaru city, HOKKAIDO 047-0013 Japan 北海道小樽市奥沢1丁目 21番15号	Sake Shochu
Kobe Shu-shin-kan 神戸酒心館	株式会社　神戸酒心館 Kobe Shu-shin-kan Breweries, Ltd www.shushinkan.co.jp	1 - 8-17 Mikagetsukamachi, Higashi-nada Ward, Kobe, HYOGO 658-0044 Japan 神戸市東灘区御影塚町 1-8-17	Sake
Mikunihare 皇国晴	皇国晴酒造　株式会社 Mikunihare Shuzo Co., Ltd www.mabotaki.co.jp	296 Ikuji, Kurobe, TOYAMA 938-0066, Japan 富山県黒部市生地296	Sake
Miyazaki Honten 宮崎本店	株式会社　宮崎本店 Miyazaki Honten Co., Ltd www.miyanoyuki.co.jp	972 Minamigomitsuka Kusu-machi Yokkaiichi City, MIE 510-0104 Japan 三重県四日市市楠町南 五味塚972	Sake Shochu Others
Nakajimaya 中島屋	株式会社　中島屋酒造場 Nakajimaya Sake Brewery http://y-shuzo.com/hp/nakajimaya.html	2-1-3 Doi, Shunan city, YAMAGUCHI 746-0011 Japan 山口県周南市土井2-1-3	Sake
Otokoyama 男山	男山　株式会社 Otokoyama Co. Ltd www.otokoyama.com	7 Nagayama 2 jo Asahikawa, HOKKAIDO, Japan 北海道旭川市永山2条 7丁目	Sake
Satsuma 薩摩	薩摩酒造　株式会社 Satsuma Shuzo Co., Ltd www.satsuma.co.jp	26 Tategamihonmachi Makurazaki KAGOSHIMA 898-0025 Japan 鹿児島県枕崎市立神本 町26	Shochu
Sekihara 関原	関原酒造　株式会社 Sekihara Shuzo Co., Ltd www.sake-sekihara.com	1-1029-1 Sekihara-cho Nagaoka city NIIGATA 940-2035 Japan 新潟県長岡市関原町1丁 目1029−1	Sake

Sudohonke 須藤本家	須藤本家　株式会社 Sudohonke Inc www.sudohonke.co.jp	2215 Obara, Kasama IBARAKI 309-1701 Japan 茨城県笠間市小原2125	Sake
Taiwakura 大和蔵	大和蔵酒造株式会社 Taiwakura Sake Brewery www.miyagisake.jp	8-1 Matsusakadaira, Taiwa-cho, Kurokawa-gun MIYAGI 981-3408 Japan 宮城県黒川郡大和町松坂平8－1	Sake
Tamanohikari 玉乃光	玉乃光酒造株式会社 Tamanohikari Sake Brewing Co., Ltd www.tamanohikari.co.jp	545 Higashisakai Machi Fushimi-ku KYOTO 612-8066 Japan 京都市伏見区東堺町545-2	Sake
Taruhei 樽平	樽平酒造株式会社 Taruhei Brewing Co., Ltd www.taruhei.co.jp	2886 Nakakomatsu Kawanishimachi (Oaza) Higashiokitama-gun YAMAGATA 999-0122 山形県東置賜郡川西町大字中小松2886	Sake
Tsukasabotan 司牡丹	司牡丹酒造　株式会社 Tsukasabotan Sake Brewing Co., Ltd www.tsukasabotan.co.jp	1299 Ko, Sakawa, Takaoka cho, KOCHI 789-1201, Japan 高知県高岡郡佐川町甲1299番地	Sake Shochu Others
Urakasumi 浦霞	株式会社　佐浦 Saura Co., Ltd www.urakasumi.com	2-19 Motomachi, Shiogama MIYAGI 985-0052 宮城県塩竈市本町2-19	Sake Shochu Others
Yoshikubo 吉久保	吉久保酒造　株式会社 Yoshikubo Sake Brewery www.ippin.co.jp	3-9-5 Honcho Mito-city IBARAKI Japan 310-0815 茨木県水戸市本町3丁目9番5号	Sake

ぶんご銘醸 株式会社 Bungo Meijyo Co., Ltd.
789-4 Naokawa Oaza Yokogawa,
Saiki, OITA 879-3105, Japan
www.bungomeijyo.co.jp

Bungo Meijyo ぶんご銘醸

Bungo Meijyo is a shochu brewery, located in Oita, Kyushu. It is surrounded by nature and the river next to the brewery always flows with clear water which is habitable for fireflies. When the summer comes fireflies fly in the night, which is an absolutely magical sight.

The brewery is not a large shochu brewery, because of this Bungo produces its own characteristic shochu with their rich resources and beautiful surroundings.

'Our Bungo has improved our skills and our intuition for a long time. In shochu brewing, we find the fermentation of Moromi mash through all of our senses to pursue the flavour and the aroma of barley. We have valued our shochu, which when matched with good food, people gather to enjoy drinking it. We have kept pursuing to brew shochu loved by people as always'.

Functional and efficient techniques are passed down in Bungo Meijyo, which enable us to produce wonderful shochu with the distinctive aromatic barley flavour.

季節になると蛍の乱舞をみることができる清流のそばに建つ蔵元。清らかな水と空気、緑豊かな森林、美しい自然の中で、小さな蔵だからできる技術で、おいしいと言われる焼酎造りにこだわっています。蔵元の長年培った、技術と勘によって五感でもろみの発酵を感じ、麦のもつうまみや香りを追及し、美味しい料理、集う人、その場の雰囲気を大切にして、自然体で飲める焼酎をこれからも造り続けていきます。

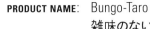

PRODUCT NAME: Bungo-Taro

雑味のないきれいな酒質で、口に含むと柔らかな甘みが広がります。ロック、水 割り、お湯割りによく合います。

DESCRIPTION: Very clear shochu, texture is mellow, and the soft sweetness of barley will spread across your tongue. We recommend having Bungo Taro Shochu with ice, water or warm water.

=〃=〃=〃=〃=〃=〃=〃=〃=〃=〃=〃=〃=〃=〃=〃=〃=〃=

香吟のささやき

PRODUCT NAME: A Whisper of Aroma

麦を50%まで精麦し、厳選した種麹と芳香を醸す酵母を使い低温発酵させた香り高い焼酎です。

DESCRIPTION: We polish barley to 50%, and choose a seed malt that gives a rich aroma. It is then fermented at a low temperature which makes the barley shochu very aromatic.

=〃=〃=〃=〃=〃=〃=〃=〃=〃=〃=〃=〃=〃=〃=〃=〃=〃=

How to drink Bungo-Shochu

Shochu is enjoyed in a variety of ways, but we recommend taking with hot or warm water. It is a common way of drinking shochu in Japan. Warm/hot water brings out the aroma and sweetness of the barley. We recommend drinking shochu with body temperature warm water at a 60:40 ratio.

Matching recommendation for our Mugi-Shochu (barley shochu)

- Chicken Tempura
- Soy Marinated sashimi of chopped Horse Mackerel and Yellowtail.

株式会社　文楽　Bunraku Co., Ltd
2 Chome-5-5 Kamicho, Ageo,
SAITAMA 362-0037, Japan
www.bunraku.net

Bunraku 文楽

The Bunraku Sake Brewery dates back to 1894, when the founder Kamekichi Kitanishi, settled in Saitama and began using the crystal clear water of the Arakawa River to produce sake.

The name Bunraku is taken from a traditional form of Japanese puppetry that involves three key actors: the puppeteer, the chanter and a shamisen player. Harmony and balance between the three is essential to this most traditional of art forms, and it is this trinity that has inspired our time-honoured method, involving three ingredients: polished rice, pure water and malted rice or koji.

Throughout over a century of history we have striven to offer the highest quality sake to our customers by strictly maintaining our ancient, traditional methods. The autumn of 2007 saw the completion of our new brewery, allowing us to harmonize traditional brewing methods with modern equipment. Yet we have fiercely defended our use of the age-old techniques that have been passed down through generations of the Kitanishi family.

The features of Bunraku sake come from brewing water drawn from the well in the garden. A little bit of hard water adds sharpness and depth of the taste of sake. Additionally, the skills of the master-brewer and the variety of rice used are essential to developing each sake's unique taste.

We seek to introduce our treasured sake to people from overseas. Having put our heart and soul into sake for over one-hundred and ten years, we can promise that our product will not be a temporary fad, but it embodies a genuine and superior element of Japanese tradition. The Bunraku brand has been in foreign countries where Japanese food is established. Traditional junmai daiginjyo, junmai-ginjyo with gold leaf for ceremonial occasions and uniquely designed bottles are very popular with foreign customers.

Buraku sake brings out the best in seasonal food. An integral part of Japanese cuisine is the consumption of typical dishes at different times of the year. We believe that Bunraku sake is the perfect sake to enjoy with traditional Japanese cuisine and for every occasion, be it an important celebration or a casual evening with friends.

=⫽=⫽=⫽=⫽=⫽=⫽=⫽=⫽=⫽=⫽=⫽=⫽=⫽=⫽=⫽=⫽=

PRODUCT NAME: Junmai Ginjyo

DESCRIPTION: Junmai Ginjyo has an excellent, harmonious combination of the rich taste from a densely compacted rice flavour along with a subtle fragrance. For centuries Japanese legend has held that gold leaf carries healing qualities which can purify the blood and protect against bad luck.

We offer this special sake for a ceremonial occasion or any special day.

Sake with an engaging umami character goes well with the delicious flavour of chicken.

=⫽=⫽=⫽=⫽=⫽=⫽=⫽=⫽=⫽=⫽=⫽=⫽=⫽=⫽=⫽=⫽=

千代むすび酒造株式会社
Chiyomusubi Sake Brewery Co., Ltd
131 Taisho-cho, Sakaiminato TOTTORI 684-0004, Japan
www.chiyomusubi.co.jp

Chiyomusubi 千代むすび

Established in 1865, we have 149 years history of sake brewing. Our brewery is located on the seaside of west Tottori prefecture that is blessed with a richness of nature. We use sake rice (Gouriki and Yamadanishiki) from the neighbourhood farmers that we know very well to make sake. 'REAL, TRUST, SAFE'.

日本酒造りは、1865年創業149年になります。四季の自然に恵まれた鳥取県西部の境港市で日本酒の製造販売を致しています。原料は、地元の鳥取県産酒造好適米（強力、山田錦）が中心で、目の見える農家の方から、直接買い付けることで、「本物、安心、安全」の日本酒を製造しています。

=ﾘ=ﾘ=ﾘ=ﾘ=ﾘ=ﾘ=ﾘ=ﾘ=ﾘ=ﾘ=ﾘ=ﾘ=ﾘ=ﾘ=ﾘ=ﾘ=ﾘ=ﾘ=ﾘ=

PRODUCT NAME: Chiyomusubi Junmai-daiginjyo
「千代むすび　純米大吟醸」

DESCRIPTION: This is the sake that we highly recommend, produced from our local grown finest rice 'Goriki'. It has a delicate aroma, rich flavour and gives a neat refreshing feeling when drinking.
リーズナブルな純米大吟醸で、強力米の、ほのかな香り、ふくよかな味わい、後味すっきりの日本酒です。

FOOD: Chiomusubi Junmai-Daiginjyo goes well with all seafood, especially dishes with snow crab (Matsuba-gani) which is a specialty of Tottori. It has juicy sweet meat that will combine well with our sake.

SERVING: Our recommended drinking temperatures for this sake are Hiya 冷 (cold: 10°C) and Kan 燗 (hot: 40°C–50°C). Chiyomusubi Junmai-Diginjyo is available in 1800 ml or 720 ml bottle.

=╱=╱=╱=╱=╱=╱=╱=╱=╱=╱=╱=╱=╱=╱=╱=╱=╱=

大七酒造株式会社
Daishichi Sake Brewery Co., Ltd
1-66 Takeda, Nihonmatsu, FUKUSHIMA 964-0902 Japan
Tel +81-243-23-0007 Fax +81-243-23-0008
www.daishichi.com
info@daishichi.com

Daishichi 大七

The Daishichi Sake Brewery Co., Ltd., located in the castle town of Nihonmatsu in Fukushima Prefecture, at the foot of majestic Mt. Adatara, has over 260 years of history. Saburoemon Ohta, who hailed originally from a samurai family, founded Daishichi in 1752. Since then, ten Ohta generations have overseen the family business. Daishichi specializes in exclusive handcrafted sakes that are very suitable for gourmet cuisine. The outstanding reputation from Daishichi's rich, mellow sakes comes from an insistence on a strictly orthodox brewing tradition: the kimoto method. Above all else, Daishichi seeks depth of flavour: sake that grows and matures over time, flowering into exceptional quality.

Grown locally, Daishichi's sake today has a worldwide appeal. Wine and food specialists from the whole world reserve the highest praise for Daishichi because of its exceptional finesse, which balances elegant refinement with a full taste and 'body.' Daishichi's sake has a unique appeal thanks to its perfect match with a variety of cuisines. Daishichi's full taste makes it a great accompaniment for main dishes, meats and dishes with buttery or creamy sauces. The Daishichi Sake Brewery regularly holds dinner parties where a full course of French food is paired with six or seven different Daishichi sakes – in Japan such events have been organized with the assistance of Shinya Tasaki, the World's Best Sommelier in 1995 and President of the Association de la Sommellerie Internationale. Recently, a similar dinner was held in Paris together with Michelin 2-star Executive Chef Eric Briffard of the Four Seasons Hotel George V.

Daishichi is served at international events such as the G8 Summit in Hokkaido, and also has featured at a Gala Dinner hosted by members of the royal family of the Netherlands. The brewery has four times acted as sponsor of the award ceremony for Dutch chefs and sommeliers of the influential Gault-Millau restaurant guide, held annually in The Hague. In 2011 Daishichi became the first Japanese sake brewery to take part with its own booth in Vinexpo, the largest wine show in the world, held every two years in Bordeaux. In the heart of the French wine country, Daishichi attracted not only tasters and buyers from many nationalities, but was also sought out by Europe's most distinguished winemakers and sommeliers.

=/=

PRODUCT NAME: Minowamon ('Minowa Gate')

GRADE: Junmai Daiginjo (very aromatic sake with full taste). Extra Super Premium sake.

TYPE: Kimoto-method

CHARACTER: Natural, elegant aroma and a gentle, mellow texture of remarkable delicacy

RICE: Yamada Nishiki

ALCOHOL: 15%

SERVING: Chill to 10–15°C.

FOOD: The crisp, clean taste of Minowamon makes it the perfect accompaniment for Japanese haute-cuisine (Kappo or Kaiseki). Also perfect with Sushi and Japanese tapas.

DESCRIPTION: This junmai daiginjo sake, brewed by the traditional kimoto method, was the first in Japan produced using the super-flat rice-polishing technique developed by Daishichi to achieve the total elimination of all components that might result in undesirable flavours. The clear taste has an underlying richness that creates a natural, elegant aroma and a gentle, mellow texture of remarkable delicacy. For many years running, this sake has gained top place in voting by *kikizakeshi* (Japanese sake sommeliers) in the refined sake section. It has also won consecutive gold medals in competitions in the United States.

=/=

PRODUCT NAME	:	Masakura ('True Cherry Blossom')
GRADE	:	Junmai Ginjo (aromatic sake with full taste). Super Premium sake.
TYPE	:	Kimoto-method
CHARACTER	:	A refreshing sake with a mild, smooth character. Has a discreet aroma and a creamy taste.
RICE	:	Gohyakumangoku
ALCOHOL	:	15%
SERVING	:	Masakura is best enjoyed lightly chilled to around 12–15°C. If you prefer, try serving it gently warmed.
FOOD	:	Masakura's gentle sweetness perfectly matches dishes with a creamy, sweet profile.

DESCRIPTION : This traditional kimoto-brewed junmai ginjo sake has a discreet fragrance that conjures up the essence of early spring. It is perfectly blended to give a well-rounded creamy flavour that is almost silky-rich. Masakura is a comforting, fresh-tasting sake with a mild flavour that is beautifully accomplished, evoking the pervading sense of calm found in a forest.

=/=/=/=/=/=/=/=/=/=/=/=/=/=/=/=/=/=/=/=

PRODUCT NAME	:	Junmai Kimoto
GRADE	:	Junmai sake (sake with full taste). Premium sake.
TYPE	:	Kimoto-method
CHARACTER	:	Rich and full bodied.
RICE	:	Gohyakumangoku
ALCOHOL	:	15%
SERVING	:	Junmai Kimoto is best appreciated at room temperature, at around 15°C, or slightly warmer. If you prefer, it can also be gently heated.
FOOD	:	The hidden depths of this sake will complement any food, but particularly creamy dishes with a gentle richness.

DESCRIPTION : Daishichi's Junmai Kimoto has achieved world renown as the definitive kimoto-brewed sake. Our master craftsmen spare no effort in creating this distinctive brew. Full maturation creates a perfect alignment of rich flavours and acidity, with a fresh, clean aftertaste. Enjoyed hot, it provides an embracing, soothing experience. The Nihon Keizai Shimbun newspaper voted our Junmai Kimoto the finest sake to drink with Japanese cuisine. It was also selected by the leading gourmet monthly magazine, Dancyu, as the best sake for drinking warm.

=/=/=/=/=/=/=/=/=/=/=/=/=/=/=/=/=/=/=/=

銀盤酒造 株式会社
Ginban Shuzo Co., Ltd.
4853-3 Ogyu, Kurobe,
TOYAMA 938-0801, Japan
www.ginban.co.jp

Ginban 銀盤

Found in 1910. We run a brewery at the foot of a 3000 metre high mountain in the Northern Alps of Toyama Prefecture.

Our sake is brewed with soft spring water originating from the mountain range. The current president rebuilt the brewery into a modern four storied building which is fully equipped with a computerized system to rationalize the production lines. It improves the environment for breweries, and these efficiencies realize price reduction while maintaining high quality sake.

The president says 'Good sake leaves no suffering after drinking' and emphasizes the importance of producing the ideal sake with the most suitable rice and techniques for polishing rice.

富山県黒部市は、三千メートル級の山が連なる北アルプスに降る雨や雪が急流となって流れ出し清冽な水に恵まれた水の都である。銀盤酒造では、酒命を宿す仕込み水に、日本名水百選にも選ばれた黒部川扇状地湧水群の軟水を使用しております。銀盤酒造（株）は、この地に明治43年に創業した。現社長は、二代目で現在の近代的な鉄筋四階建ての蔵元にした。

蔵内を見ると各部署にコンピューター制御、さまざまな醸造機械、大型タンクなどが整備されている。社長は、無駄仕事を止め合理的にと機械化を強調する。

「飲んで頭の痛くなる酒は駄目だ」と酒造好適米の使用と精白度を上げることを指示する。よって、吟醸、純米大吟醸が次々と誕生し、特に「米の芯」が大人気となり銀盤の名声が上昇した。

=//=//=//=//=//=//=//=//=//=//=//=//=//=//=//=//=//=//=//=

PRODUCT NAME: Kome no Shin Daiginjyo 米の芯大吟醸

DESCRIPTION: Ginban brewery is famous for our flagship sake Ginban 'Kome No shin, Junmai Daiginjyo'. 'Kome no Shin' literary means 'the core of rice, which is polished rice'.

This sake is stored in a low temperature for a long period time (-2°C--5°C). This process gives a rich aroma to this clear and dry sake. When you sip 'Kome no Shin', a rich bouquet will go through your nose. This sake complements a delicate tasting fish such as flounder dish.

合同酒精 株式会社
Godo Shusei Co., Ltd
6-2-10 Ginza, Chuo-ku, TOKYO 104-8162 Japan
www.oenon.jp/company/group/godo.html

Godo Shusei 合同酒精

Our sake is distilled with a Japanese herb 'Shiso' (red perilla) and pure water sourced from the mountain in Hokkaido. The delicate aroma of Shiso and it's clear taste offer a pleasant experience to enjoy shochu spirits.

HOW TO DRINK: Usually enjoyed with ice or soda. Also as a cocktail 'Shiso Mojito' (mix of TAN TAKA TAN, Shiso leaves, lime, soda and sugar)

FOOD: TAN TAKA TAN would pair perfectly with Sashimi.

Tatsuuma-Honke Brewing Co. Ltd
辰馬本家酒造株式会社
8-21 Kurakakecho, Nishinomiya,
HYOGO 662-0926, Japan
www.hakushika.co.jp

Hakushika 白鹿

Hakushika (Tatsuuma-Honke)

Founded in 1662, Tatsuuma-Honke Shuzo brewery has a long history going back over 350 years. Our sakes, Kuromatsu-Hakushika and Hakushika are brewed through extensive tradition and are created with prayers for your long and calm enjoyable life.

   The base of sake comes from nature such as rice, water and wind. Therefore we brew our sake in harmony with nature.

   As it was in the past, Hakushika is brewed today in the rich climate of Nishinomiya using its natural resources such as Miyamizu (the most famous water supply related to sake), high quality rice and the air from the sea and winds from Mt. Rokko.

   Great sake can only come from rich nature. Sake is referred to as 'Life water' in Japan. It was developed by the favour of Mother Nature. It is our secure belief that we are not making the sake but merely bringing the sake to life from the natural ingredients by carefully taking our time and deep affection.

辰馬本家酒造は、1662年に創業し350年以上の歴史を持ち、清酒「黒松白鹿」「白鹿」は、日本酒づくりの基本である米、水、風といった自然と対話しながら伝統と創造を積み重ね、おおらかに楽しむ酒、長生を祈る酒を醸しています。白鹿の酒づくりを支えているのは今も昔も、西宮という豊かな風土　－　宮水、良質の米、摂海の温気、六甲おろし。良い酒は、自然の恵み豊かな風土にしか生まれません。酒は生命の水とも言われるように、大いなる自然の恵みと生命（酵母）の営みによって生まれてきます。愛情をこめて、麹や酵母のたくましい成長を見守り育てていくのが白鹿の酒づくりです。「酒はつくるものではなく、ゆっくりと時間と愛情をかけて、育てるもの。」　　　それがしなやかな技とともに、これからも脈々と受け継いでいくのが白鹿の信条です。

PRODUCT NAME:	Goka Sennenju Junmai Daiginjo 豪華千年壽 純米大吟醸
TYPE:	Junmai Daiginjo
ALC/VOL:	15.7%
RICE POLISHING RATE:	50%
RICE VARIETIES:	Yamadanishiki, Nihonbare
NIHON SHUDO (SAKE METER):	0 (neutral)
SERVING TEMPERATURE:	Chilled or room temperature

=╱=╱=╱=╱=╱=╱=╱=╱=╱=╱=╱=╱=╱=╱=╱=╱=╱=

To make our sake, we first carefully select the rice, then polish away 50% of the rice. We follow the Kakutsuru's traditional method of steaming the rice and brew the sake with Miyamizu. This sake has a fragrance of fruits and a rich body derived from the characteristics of the rice and water. Our sake was awarded the 'gold prize' by the Monde Selection in 2009, 2010 and 2011. Hakushika's Junmai-Daiginjo has a refreshing and elegant taste. Our Ginjyo sake has rich Umami flavour that goes well with simple seasonal dishes bringing out the rich flavour of the ingredients.

山田錦等の酒米を長時間かけて、精米歩合50%まで磨きあげ、天与の名水、西宮の「宮水」と白鹿伝承蒸米仕込でじっくり醸しました。それぞれの特性を引き出した珠玉の逸品は、果実にも似た爽やかな香り（吟醸香）とやわらかで、しかも深みのある味わい。奏でるハーモニーをお愉しみください。
2009年・2010年・2011年、三年連続モンドセレクション最高金賞受賞。
白鹿の純米大吟醸酒は、爽やかな飲み口と上品な旨みを楽しめるお酒。吟醸造りながら旨みが十分に感じられる酒には、しっかりとした旨みを持つ食材の味を生かした、シンプルな味付けの料理がおすすめです。

Kobe-gyu no Tataki with ponzu-vinaigrette

'Kobe-gyu' is one of the greatest beef in Japan. Kobe beef is popular and widely known by all over the world. Kobe beef is not just a kind of beef; it was selected beef from Tajima wagyubeef that are grown in Hyogo Prefecture. The deep and delicate flavours of our Junmai Daiginjo Sake goes well with the world renowned Kobe beef, served with citrus soy sauce which adds a refreshing taste and refined sourness to the beef.

白鶴酒造 株式会社
Hakutsuru Sake Brewing Co., Ltd
4-5-5 Sumiyoshi Minamimachi Higashinada Ward,
Kobe HYOGO 658-0041 Japan
http://www.hakutsuru.co.jp

Hakutsuru 白鶴

The Hakutsuru Sake Brewing Company, since it's founding in 1743, has supported the food life and social culture of people everywhere. 'To friendship for all time', this slogan expresses the spirit that Hakutsuru Sake embodies in our approach to making good sake from generation to generation. It is meant to express our constant devotion to the craft and to the promotion of sake in culinary culture.

Hakutsuru Sake Brewing Co., Ltd. is located in the Nada district of Kobe, a leading sake production centre known throughout Japan. The Nada district has high-quality natural spring water and cold winters – two ideal elements for brewing sake. Also, the hometown to a craftsman's guild for sake brewers from the region, known as Tamba toji, is located nearby. The brewers' superior skills have certainly been an important factor in the sake's quality.

「時をこえ、親しみの心をおくる」
当社はこのスローガンのもと、1743年の創業以来みなさまの食文化、生活文化を応援してまいりました。酒造りには良質の米、水が欠かせません。当社所在地である神戸周辺は酒米の王様と呼ばれる「山田錦」や六甲山系の自然水に恵まれています。

=∥=∥=∥=∥=∥=∥=∥=∥=∥=∥=∥=∥=∥=∥=∥=∥=∥=∥=

PRODUCT NAME: Junmai-Daiginjyo Sho-une　純米大吟醸　翔雲

DESCRIPTION: The 'Ginjo' among the 'Ginjo' sake varieties is a very luxurious alcohol in which the rice is polished and processed to half (or more than half) of its size. Very delicate and skilled techniques are necessary for preparation, as it is said to be a masterpiece of sake showing the skills of a master sake brewer.

　　Sho-une (soaring cloud) is a high-quality premium sake brewed with Nada's spring water, produced only from 'Yamada-nishiki,' the king of 'Sakamai (sake-making rice),' making the best of expert skills of 'Tamba-Toji' (master of sake brewer) and state-of-the-art brewing technology. Sho-une with fruity aromas and velvety smoothness can be enjoyed both chilled and at room temperature.

FOOD: Kobe-gyu, one of the most popular ingredients in Kobe goes well with Sho-une. The fine flesh with gorgeous marbling enhances its rich flavour with Sho-une.

神戸を代表する食材、「神戸牛」。上品な甘みのある赤み、繊細な霜降りが特徴の神戸牛と翔雲との相性は抜群です。ワイングラスに注いでいただくとより一層大吟醸の華やかな香りをお楽しみいただけます。

=╱=╲=╱=╲=╱=╲=╱=╲=╱=╲=╱=╲=╱=╲=╱=╲=╱=╲=╱=╲=╱=╲=╱=╲=╱=

株式会社　今西清兵衛商店
S. Imanishi Co., Ltd
4-1 Fukuchi in-cho, Nara-city
NARA 630-8381 JAPAN
www.harushika.com

Harushika 春鹿

Nara is not only the first cosmopolitan city in Japan, but also the birthplace of sake production, as it is known today. Established in 1884, Harushika is located in the Nara town in which there are some World Heritage Sites; Todaiji Temple, Kasuga Shrine, etc. Legend says gods gave the name to this sake brewery. The present sake production is based on the traditional sake brewing technologies in Nara. The basic policy of Harushika is, from the beginning, to transmit those technologies.

Mr. Furukawa, a Toji, the chief brewer at Harushika, mentions, *'Polishing sake rice, polishing water, polishing skills and polishing mental strength are the basic motto when working as Toji'*. Furthermore, he believes in caring about the ingredients, such as malt, yeast and also the environment, for all these elements go into producing good quality sake.

日本最初の国際都市「奈良」からうまれた「南都諸白」の伝統を現在に伝える。日本で最初の国際都市「奈良」は日本酒発祥の地といわれています。今西家はこの地で明治１７年（1884年）より酒造業を始めました。　蔵元は春日大社や東大寺などの世界遺産にほど近い、昔の風情を残す奈良町にございます。明治17年（1884年）に酒造業を創業。酒銘は、春日の神々が鹿に乗ってやってきたという伝説から、「春日神鹿（かすがしんろく）」と名付け、後に「春鹿（はるしか）」に改め、今日に至る。また酒母造りの原型である「菩提酛」や、玄米を白米仕込みにする「

諸白造り」の革新が、日本の酒造りの根幹となっている。味、コク、香りと全ての点で高品質となり、全国に名声が轟いた「南都諸白（なんともろはく）」の伝統を伝えていくことを創業以来の精神としている。

杜氏の言葉　古川武志
「米を磨く」、「水を磨く」、「技を磨く」、「心を磨く」のお基本理念の基、造り手、麹、酵母をはじめ、全てに良い環境づくりをする事が、良い酒造り、旨い酒に繋がると思っております。

'Our tradition is to innovate'. Under this the Harushika's family motto, Harushika is known as the first brewery that brewed and sold the extra dry sake. At the same time the brewery is known for their light and well-finished sake, which has a brilliant aroma and smooth texture. In recent years, they have produced a low alcohol sparkling sake, and restored the wooden barrower for brewing that gives rich flavour to sake.

『春鹿』は、「伝統とは革新にあり」の家訓の下、酵母の限界に挑戦した純米超辛口酒を醸造し、大々的に発売した全国最初の酒蔵として有名。全商品の95％を純米酒・吟醸酒・大吟醸が占め、軽快で切れ味の良い酒、華やかでまろやかな口当たりの酒を醸している。また、低アルコール発泡純米酒の醸造や、木桶発祥の地である「奈良」で濃醇な味わいの木桶仕込みのお酒も復活させた。

═╬═

PRODUCT NAME: Harushika, Junmail Chokarakuchi 春鹿　純米超辛口

DESCRIPTION: This sake is a representative brand of Harushika, and drunk in dozens of countries, such as America, Europe, etc. The brewer produces this top grade dry sake with their traditional brewing technologies. It has a soft aroma, smooth texture, and it is extra dry yet shows hints of sweetness of the rice on the palate. All of these elements are very balanced and it is great with food. Kan (warm/hot) style is also an enjoyable way for serving.

MATCHING DISHES: Delicate fish dishes such as snapper sashimi, fresh oyster, Yakitori with salt (skewered chicken with salt), tempura.

アメリカ、ヨーロッパ、アジアをはじめとする10数カ国でも愛飲されている春鹿の代表銘柄。
伝統ある技術が生んだ究極の辛口酒。見事に調和したコクとキレは、お料理との相性抜群。
口は辛いというよりは甘みが少ないお酒。穏やかな香り、甘さを抑えた　まろやかな口
料理例：鯛などの白身魚の刺身、生牡蠣、イカの刺身、焼き鳥(塩)、てんぷら
お燗もオお燗もオススメです。

═╬═

PRODUCT NAME: Tokimeki, Harushika Happo-junmaishu
ときめき　春鹿　発泡純米酒

DESCRIPTION: Tokimeki means 'excitement in love'. This sparkling sake can be drunk as a sweet Champagne. It has the harmony of the mellow sweetness of rice and the refreshing sparkling of yeast, creating a superb combination. It is recommended to chill in ice, and have in a flute glass. Adding a slice of lime adds more freshness. It is ok to drink in fruit cocktails.

ぷちぷちスウィートなお酒のしゃんぱんです。米のふくよかな甘みと酵母が奏でる爽やかな泡が絶妙のハーモニーを演出します。シャンパンと同じく氷水キリッと冷やしてシャンパングラスで。ライムを少し加えるとより爽やかに。カットしたイチゴを入れてお洒落にお楽しみ下さい。数種類の果実を細かく刻んでフルーツをカクテルもオススメです。

PRODUCT NAME: Harushika Junmai-Daiginjo 春鹿　純米大吟醸

DESCRIPTION: Yamadanishiki rice is polished 50% and brewed at a low temperature, giving a brilliant aroma, soft umami, and sweetness of rice. It is a smooth and superior quality sake.

MATCHING DISHES: Scallop sashimi, Lobster sashimi, stirred mushrooms, etc.

PRODUCT NAME: Harushika Sakura Junmai-shu 春鹿　さくらラベル　純米酒

DESCRIPTION: With a soft and delicate nose, silky texture. Sweet and soft umami spread across your tongue quickly.

MATCHING DISHES: Sukiyaki, Yakitori with teriyaki, Oden, Miso-dengaku, squid and sea urchin, etc

穏やかな香りと柔らかな口当たり。お米の甘く優しい旨味とコクが口中に広がる。

PRODUCT NAME: Harushika Junmai-ginjo 春鹿　純米吟醸

DESCRIPTION: Flowery aroma to the nose. Full-bodied and rich umami with a great finish that is quite clean. As these elements suggest, this sake is constructed to match perfectly with food.

MATCHING DISHES: Oyster, Cuttlefish sashimi, Grilled crab, etc

華やかな香りが広がり、まったりとした米の旨味、後口はすっきりしたキレ味。料理と絶妙のハーモニーを奏でます。

株式会社 一ノ蔵 Ichinokura Co., Ltd
14 Okeyaki, Matsuyama Sengoku, Osaki city
MIYAGI 987-1393 Japan
www.ichinokura.co.jp
TEL: 0229-55-3322 FAX0229-55-4513
E-MAIL: sake@ichinokura.co.jp

Ichinokura 一ノ蔵

Ichinokura, a sake brewery in Miyagi Prefecture, northern part of Japan, was established in 1973 by merging with four historic breweries. Our brand Ichinokura was named after three of our wishes: 1) to become the number one brewery 2) to exist as a unique brewery 3) four founders to unite into one brewery.

Our main brewery in Matsuyama, a part of Osaki city in Miyagi Prefecture, is surrounded by forest with clean and fresh air and blessed with abundant underground water and rice suitable for sake making. We have continued to brew traditionally genuine sake and revolutionary new types of sake.

Rice for sake brewing

Miyagi Prefecture is well known for quality rice in Japan. Ichinokura sake is made with rice harvested mainly in Miyagi Prefecture. We also have promoted use of environmentally friendly rice for sake brewing. Ichinokura Nosha, an agricultural department, was organized in cooperation with local farmers in 2004 and Ichinokura started producing rice by environmentally friendly methods.

Expertise of Ichinokura

One of the most important factors in sake brewing is the expertise of Kurabito, brewery workers. They are led by a Toji who is their head master of Kurabito and experienced in sake brewing technology of the Nanbu Toji School. Ichinokura has over 40 brewery workers. They devote themselves to brew sake day and night with their quest for excellence during sake brewing season. While maintaining the traditional expertise, Ichinokura also keep challenging themselves to create new types of sake such as sparkling sake Suzune. Ichinokura sake has been brewed by a well-balanced way between high-tech and low-tech.

PRODUCT NAME:	Ichinokura Junmai Daiginjo Kuranohana 一ノ蔵　純米大吟醸蔵の華
DESCRIPTION:	Elegant mild, light-bodied with refined fruity sweet aroma. It is made with 40% polished rice, harvested in Miyagi-pref, locally.
ALCOHOL CONTENT:	15%
RICE POLISHING RATIO:	40%
RICE VARIETY:	Kuranohana
SERVING:	8–18°C
MATCHING DISHES:	White meat fish sashimi, Yakitori with salt, Tempura with salt, Vinegared snow crab

PRODUCT NAME:	Ichinokura Tokubetsu Junmaishu Karakuchi 一ノ蔵　特別純米酒辛口
DESCRIPTION:	This is the most popular sake among the junmaishu (pure rice sake) category of Ichinokura products. Light and smooth, with the aroma of grains and a touch of mineral. Round taste with a full rice flavor and refined dryness.
ALCOHOL CONTENT:	15%
RICE POLISHING RATIO:	55%
RICE VARIETY:	Sasanishiki, Kuranohana
SERVING:	Chilled, Room temperature, Warm
MATCHING DISHES:	Sake steamed clam or scallop, tempura of shrimp, gratin, fried oyster, yakitori

=⫟=⫟=⫟=⫟=⫟=⫟=⫟=⫟=⫟=⫟=⫟=⫟=⫟=⫟=⫟=⫟=⫟=⫟=

PRODUCT NAME:	Ichinokura Suzune Wabi 一ノ蔵　すず音 Wabi
DESCRIPTION:	Sweet sparkling sake just brewed with rice. Elegantly smooth it gives a refreshing sweet taste with fruity aromas.
ALCOHOL CONTENT:	5%
RICE POLISHING RATIO:	65%
RICE VARIETY:	Shunyo, Toyonishiki
SERVING:	4–6 °C
MATCHING DISHES:	Cheese, gratin, California roll, yakitori, teriyaki, ceasar salad, fresh fruits

=⫟=⫟=⫟=⫟=⫟=⫟=⫟=⫟=⫟=⫟=⫟=⫟=⫟=⫟=⫟=⫟=⫟=⫟=

株式会社　一本義久保本店
Ippongi Kubo Honten Co.,Ltd
1-3-1 Sawa machi, Katsuyama City
FUKUI 911-8585 Japan
www.ippongi.co.jp

IPPONGI 一本義

Ippongi Sake Brewery is located in one of Japan's best rice growing regions, Katsuyama City, Fukui Prefecture, a town nestled in the foothills of Mt. Hakusan (lit. White mountain) known for its deep winter snows. Katsuyama is called the Dinosaur Kingdom, as more dinosaur fossils have been excavated here than in any other region in Japan. Katsuyama City and neighbouring Ono City make up the region called Oku-Echizen. The region is blessed with pure water, fertile soil, and an ideal temperature difference between night and day, creating the perfect environment to grow large amounts of high quality sake rice.

Oku-Echizen is known by sake brewers for being one of the most productive areas in Japan for the sake rice, 'Gohyakumangoku'. In addition, the famous 'Yamadanishiki' and newly developed sake rice, 'Koshinoshizuku' are also grown here. 'Koshinoshizuku' is a very rare type of sake rice that first appeared in 2003 and has not been distributed anywhere outside of Fukui Prefecture. It allows the production of only 1000 bales a year.

In Ippongi's Denshin series, 'Koshinoshizuku' is used for 'RIN/ Air of the brewery' and 'INE/ Rice field', and a blend of 'Yamadanishiki' and 'Gohyakumangoku' is used for 'Yuki/Snow'. In the days when samurai still roamed the streets, feudal lord of Katsuyama, Lord Ogasawara, gave the symbolic name 'Ippongi' to the sake brewed exclusively for him.

The name 'Ippongi' comes from the Zen term 'Daiichigitai', which means ultimate truth.

When Ippongi Sake Brewery was founded in 1902, the company inherited this historical sake name.

Since the beginning, Ippongi has been brewing high-quality dry sake. Within 10 years of its founding, it became the top brand in Fukui Prefecture, a position it continues to hold to this day, nearly 100 years later. Around the 1950s, having already made a name for itself with its excellent dry sake, Ippongi began to seek a way to create an even more elegant and refined taste. The taste Ippongi was aiming for was something pure with a beautifully articulated fragrance and flavour. To accomplish this, Ippongi turned to the Nanbu brewing method (developed among brew masters from southern Iwate Prefecture, which was famous for producing sake with a clean, clear taste). The company began employing a toji (brew master) well-versed in the Nanbu methods, and since then Ippongi has consistently worked to produce a quality sake which embodies these ideals of purity in both taste and fragrance. In the 89th Nanbu-Toji Sake Contest (2007), Ippongi won the grand prize out of 586 contestants, thus attaining the highest possible honor among all sake brewed with the Nanbu method.

About the Nanbu-Toji Association

The Nanbu-Toji Association is one of the three most excellent brew master associations in Japan along with Echigo-toji and Tanba-toji. Of this esteemed triumvirate, Nanbu-Toji is widely considered to be the best. It has a history of over 350 years, and the skills and craftsmanship of the Nanbu-Toji Association have been praised throughout the history of sake brewing.

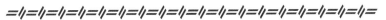

PRODUCT NAME: Denshin Rin ~air of the brewery~ 伝心 凜

DESCRIPTION: This is a Junmai Daiginjo sake with a rich aroma that carries undertones of peaches and lychee and an elegant taste full of depth and freshness. This sake is brewed solely using 'Koshinoshizuku' which is a very rare sake rice produced only in Fukui Prefecture.

MATCHING DISHES: Dish with sour dressing. Vinaigrette salad. Dried fruits, cherry, etc.

PRODUCT NAME: Denshin Yuki ~snow~ 伝心 雪

DESCRIPTION: This sake features a calm fragrance and pure crisp taste that gives you a sense of a quiet, snow-covered sake factory. Denshin Yuki's tranquil aroma and clear taste has garnered enthusiastic support not only from customers who enjoy a pure-tasting sake, but also from chefs who seek a sake that finely accompanies delicate cuisine.

MATCHING DISHES: Chicken kara-age. Fatty fish ■中トロなど油系の刺身

═〃═〃═〃═〃═〃═〃═〃═〃═〃═〃═〃═〃═〃═〃═〃═

PRODUCT NAME: Denshin Ine ~rice field~ 伝心 稲

DESCRIPTION: This sake features a smooth feeling with a soft dry taste that gives you a sense of fully ripe rice plants swaying gently in the breeze. This sake is brewed solely using 'Koshi no Shizuku' which is a very rare sake rice produced only in Fukui Prefecture.

MATCHING DISHES: Dashimaki-tamago. Grilled eel. Chawan-mushi.

═〃═〃═〃═〃═〃═〃═〃═〃═〃═〃═〃═〃═〃═〃═〃═

PRODUCT NAME: Ginkoubai Hannya Tou 吟香梅 般若刀

DESCRIPTION: Take a sip, and following the initial full-bodied sweetness enjoy the bold spicy flavour that spreads through your mouth. Guaranteed, before now you've never experienced a flavour quite like this. Just one drink and you'll be hooked, and wanting to recommend it to all of your friends.

MATCHING DISHES: Beef dishes. Yogurt. Avocado, avocado roll.

═〃═〃═〃═〃═〃═〃═〃═〃═〃═〃═〃═〃═〃═〃═〃═

Product	Chilled	Room temp.	Warm	Hot
RIN	☆☆☆	☆☆	—	☆☆
YUKI	☆☆☆	☆☆	☆☆	☆
INE	☆☆☆	☆☆	☆☆☆	☆☆
GINKOUBAI HANNYA TOU	☆☆	☆☆☆	—	—

This chart shows the best temperatures to enjoy the above sake. Stars indicates the preference.
— area is not recommend.

越前仕立て汐雲丹（越前うに）

江戸時代の越前福井では、越前仕立て汐雲丹（えちぜんしたてしおうに）は各浜の漁師たちの浜の年貢の一つとして作られ、旧福井藩に納められておりました。また旧福井藩に納めた汐雲丹は、軍事用の備蓄食や各宮家・他藩への贈物としていたようです。
さまざまに贈られる品々の中でも「長崎奉行の持品のからすみ」「尾張公の持品のこのわた」「　越前公の持品の越前の雲丹」。この三品は美味である上、いずれも大量製造ができず入手が困難であったことにより、江戸時代より日本三大珍味と称されております。
天たつは、旧越前福井藩　松平家の御用商として代々この越前仕立て汐雲丹を一手にとりまとめておりましたが、この頃は一般の方との取引は禁じられておりました。古来より希少な高級珍味として人々に愛され、一部の限られた方だけに食されており、現在のように広く一般の方への販売、お召上がり頂くように　なったのは明治以降になってからです。
雲丹の古くは奈良時代に、若狭の国より朝廷に贈られた様です。江戸時代に塩蔵法が考案されるまでの雲丹は、今よりも水分が多く「泥うに」と呼ばれ、ひしゃくですくっていた為、瀬戸焼のうに鉢にいれられていました。

江戸時代になり「塩蔵法」による越前仕立て汐雲丹の製法が考案。軍事用の保存携帯説明食として、また朝廷や幕府の各藩への贈り物にも使われておりました。越前仕立て汐雲丹の製法「塩蔵法」の考案は、当店の創業より数えて三代目当主・天野五兵衛の代（2011年現在で10代目）。
当時の福井藩主の松平治好公から、「日持ちのする　うにの貯蔵品を作るように」と命じた天たつの三代目当主・天野五兵衛が、現在まで続く「塩蔵法」による越前仕立て汐雲丹を考案し、その「塩蔵法」を越前海岸一帯に広めたと言われております。
天たつの越前仕立て汐うにの原料は、日本海沿岸でとれた国産ばふんうにの卵巣のみを使用いたしております。天たつの越前仕立て汐雲丹は、江戸時代より伝わる「塩蔵法」にて、「ばふんうにの卵巣」と「塩」だけで仕上げております。余分なものは一切加えておりません。100gの製品を仕上げるのに100個以上のばふんうにの卵巣を使用しておりますので、ねっとりと濃厚で峻烈な味わいです。
「上あごの裏に小豆粒くらいの量の汐雲丹をつけてそれをなめながらお酒を一合飲む」というのが粋なお酒の飲み方だといわれております。濃厚な味なので乾いた箸か爪楊枝の先に小指の先ほどつけてお召し上がりください。日本酒のお供にとてもよく合います。また、炊き立てのご飯の上に乗せるととろりととけて、磯の風味がひろがり美味です。焼き海苔にまいて食べても美味しいです。焼いたトーストに塗って頂いても美味です。
　古くから三大珍味として愛されている天たつの越前仕立て汐雲丹。手土産に、大切なご友人との酒宴にも、粋で贅沢な酒肴として　おすすめです。

神楽酒造 株式会社 Kagura Shuzo Co., Ltd
144-1 Iwato, Takachiho, Nishiusuki District,
MIYAZAKI 882-1621, Japan
http://www.kagurashuzo.co.jp

Kagura 神楽

Kagura Shuzo Co., Ltd. is a leading shochu company in Japan. We produce our genuine shochu made from carefully selected raw materials; especially barley, rice and ume plum are 100% domestic. Surrounded by abundant natural resources, we continue to make our high quality products.

Kagura brewery was established in 1954, in Takachiho town, Miyazaki Prefecture. Since inauguration, with the motto 'Producing and delivering superior shochu to customers', we have produced our product toward building a brand that would be loved by people. In addition, in 2009, a new plant was opened in Saito city that is famous for beautiful water and producing quality shochu sweet potatoes. Selected ingredients, warm climate, brilliant sun, our shochu is blessed with a beautiful natural environment, and these products are well liked by drinkers in Japan.

蔵元の紹介…神楽酒造は昭和29年、神話のふるさと宮崎県高千穂町にて創業し、以来常に品質の向上を図り、「優れた焼酎をお客様にお届けする事」を社是として、愛される商品づくりを目指して参りました。平成21年、宮崎県西都市の清冽な西都清水（さいときよみず）に出会い、芋づくりの盛んな西都の地で新工場を操業させました。
厳選された原料、温暖な気候、燦々と降り注ぐ太陽、この豊かな環境で育まれた焼酎は、日本中の愛飲家の賞賛を受け、親しまれています。

=〟=〟=〟=〟=〟=〟=〟=〟=〟=〟=〟=〟=〟=〟=〟=〟=〟=

PRODUCT NAME: 天孫降臨 (TENSONKOURIN)
Tensonkourin 25% 720ml (Sweet potato shochu)

DESCRIPTION: Made from selected sweet potatoes. The mild and light taste makes it easy to drink.
   This shochu is produced with the low-temperature distillation. It prevents excessive heating, and brings out properties of sweet potato, and gives a flowery aroma. Recommended to have with ice.

SERVING: Enjoy on the rocks or with hot water.
酒質…芋焼酎では珍しい「減圧蒸留」を施す事で華やか且つスッキリとした香味を引き出す事に成功した。本格焼酎はモロミ（醗酵した原料）を沸騰させてアルコールを抽出する蒸留酒です。通常の常圧蒸留法は約100度で沸騰しますが、低温蒸留法は蒸留機内の気圧を下げて48度〜55度の低温で行い、熱による変化を抑えることができます。
　『天孫降臨』は、この低温蒸留法により、原料のさつまいも本来の香りと旨味、そして華やかな香りを選りすぐって引き出すことに成功しました。

MATCHING DISHES: Grilled Caracoled Chicken
Sashimi, Kara-age, hot pot, etc

=⫽=⫽=⫽=⫽=⫽=⫽=⫽=⫽=⫽=⫽=⫽=⫽=⫽=⫽=⫽=⫽=⫽=⫽=

PRODUCT NAME: Himukano Kurouma　くろうま長期貯蔵

ALCOHOL CONTENT: 25%

DESCRIPTION: Made from barley and barley-koji. Aged more than three years in oak barrels, which creates a rich and mature fragrance and flavour.
Enjoy straight or on the rocks.
国産二条大麦100%使用の本格麦焼酎「くろうま」を樽で長期間熟成させた長期貯蔵酒。
琥珀色の豊かな香りと深いまろやかな味わいをお楽しみください。ロックが最適ですが、コーラで割ってもおいしくいただけます

=⫽=⫽=⫽=⫽=⫽=⫽=⫽=⫽=⫽=⫽=⫽=⫽=⫽=⫽=⫽=⫽=⫽=⫽=

木戸泉酒造 株式会社
Kidoizumi Shuzo Co., Ltd
7635-1 Ohara, Isumi city,
Chiba prefecture, 298-0004 Japan
http://kidoizumi.jpn.com/

Kidoizumi 木戸泉

Founded in 1879, Kidoizumi realized the risk of preservatives and additives at an early stage, and developed their own natural sake yeast. This is stored for a long period to mature under natural conditions. Since then they have always been concerned about natural brewing using organic ingredients.

創業明治12年（1879年）。昭和30年前後、日本酒に保存料を添加されていたサリチル酸の毒性にいち早く気づき、保存料の添加を廃止するとともに独自の酒母造りを開発する。この酒母により日本酒の長期熟成の実験に入り、昭和46年、長期熟成酒「オールド木戸泉」を発売。添加物や農薬、化学肥料を一切使用しない日本酒を造りたいという先代の強い意志から昭和42年より自然農法産米を100％使用した純米酒の製造を始める。

=//=//=//=//=//=//=//=//=//=//=//=//=//=//=//=

PRODUCT NAME: Shizenmai Junmaishu　自然舞 純米酒

DESCRIPTION: Shizenmai is made with organic rice and naturally brewed. To harness the power and greatness of the land, our sake rice is farmed organically using organic plant fertilizer. We do not use agricultural chemicals, chemical fertilizers or animal fertilizers. Also in the brewing method, we only use Koji, (aspergillum), yeast and lactic acid bacterium from nature, and allow the sake to ferment naturally without pruning.

This sake is first soft to the tongue then has a refreshing sour feel. Followed with body and umami, it smoothly passes through the throat. It is a very healthy style of sake, as there is generally no hangover.

Another characteristic is that the quality of the sake is maintained for a long period of time. As it gains in maturity in the barrels the sake develops a deep amber tint and a smooth texture. We have been brewing this since 1967, Shizenmai is our masterpiece.

RICE POLISHED RATIO: 65%

ALCOHOL CONTENT: 16.50% by volume

PRODUCT NAME: Kidoizumi Junmai Daigo　木戸泉 純米醍醐

DESCRIPTION: Rich flowery acidity brought out by natural lactic acid enhances the umami in the sake. Can be drunk cold or at room temperature, but the recommended is lukewarm like the natural body temperature.

RICE POLISHED RATIO: 60%

ALCOHOL CONTENT: 16.50% by volume

木戸泉 KIDOIZUMI

北の誉酒造　株式会社
Kitanohomare Shuzo Co., Ltd
1-21-15 Okusawa, Otaru city,
HOKKAIDO 047-0013 Japan
www.kitanohomare.com

Kitanohomare 北の誉

Kitanohomare Brewery was founded in 1901 in Otaru, Hokkaido the northern island of Japan. Otaru is famous through Japan for its excellent water sauce.

The founder, Mr Kichijiro Noguchi named his brewery 'KITANO HOMARE', it translates to 'the North praise'. But 'KITANO HOMARE' the name is reflected by Mr. Noguch's expectations as a brewer, *'Here in the Northern part of Japan, be praised/ admired men, produce praised sake and be a praised Sakagura (sake brewery)'*. Sake is an important part of Japanese culture. It has been used for rites and festivals from time immemorial and also plays an efficient role as a communication tool in social situations. However in some cases, drinking alcohol can be harmful and it can lead people to take risks and put themselves into anti-social situations.

Mr. Noguchi was concerned about the responsibility to be a reliable sake brewer under the name of 'Kitanohomare', holding their pride and persistent efforts to pursuing their premium sake.

北の誉酒造の創業は1901年。蔵を構えた場所は早くから名水の地として知られていた小樽。「北の誉」の命名には「この北の地で、褒め称えられる人、褒め称えられる酒、褒め称えられる地酒であろう」との思いが込められています。

「北の誉」の由来
日本酒は古来より、神事や祭事など本人の文化や生活に深くかかわりを持つとともに、人と人との円滑にするコミュニケーションツールとしての役割を果たしています。ただ、その一方ではお酒は飲みすぎで醜態をさらしたり、人を狂わせたり破綻材料にもなりかねません。創業者の野口吉次朗は、お酒がそのような飲まれ方にならないように、お酒を造る人や酒蔵が皆様から誇れるような立場でありたいとの思いをこめ「この北の地で、褒め称えられる人、褒め称えられる酒、褒め称えられる地酒であろう」との意味で命名したと伝えられています。

=〟=〟=〟=〟=〟=〟=〟=〟=〟=〟=〟=〟=〟=〟=〟=〟=〟=〟=

PRODUCT NAME: Junmai genshu SAMURAI 純米原酒　侍

DESCRIPTION: Junmai Ginjo SAMURAI is made using traditional techniques. This sake is brewed using the finest locally grown Sakamai (rice for sake) called GINPUU. 40% of the rice is polished away to make this sake 'Junnmai-shu. This sake has a richness and UMAMI (taste), which is derived from the rice. Also it has the characteristic powerful taste of Genshu, which means undiluted sake (most sake are slightly diluted).

SAMURAI can be enjoyed served over a wide range of temperatures from chilled to warm. You can also enjoy as a cocktail, SAMURAI Rock (mixed with citrus juice and ice cubes). This sake goes well with hairy crab, which is a specialty product of Hokkaido (Northern island of Japan) area. Hairy crab has graceful and willowy meat with a rich taste of crab butter. Pour the sake into a crab shell then you can enjoy so called 'Kani-no koura sake' as well.

北海道産の酒造好適米「吟風」を精米歩合６０％まで磨き、伝統の字で醸した「純米原酒侍」は、米のうまみとコクに加え、原酒ならではの力強い味わいのお酒です。
冷から燗まで幅広い温度帯でお楽しみいただけますが、柚子やライム果汁を入れたサムライロックもおすすめです。
北海道の味覚を代表する毛蟹との相性も良く、しなやかで繊細な身と濃厚な蟹味噌の他、蟹の甲羅に日本酒を注ぐ「カニの甲羅酒」としても楽しむ方法もあります。

=〟=〟=〟=〟=〟=〟=〟=〟=〟=〟=〟=〟=〟=〟=〟=〟=〟=〟=

株式会社　神戸酒心館
Kobe Shu-shin-kan Breweries, Ltd
1 - 8-17 Mikagetsukamachi, Higashi-nada Ward,
Kobe, HYOGO 658-0044 Japan
www.shushinkan.co.jp

Kobe Shu-shin-kan 神戸酒心館

Kobe Shu-shin-kan founded in 1751, is located in the district of Kobe situated in the rich and beautiful natural environment of Nada, Mikage surrounded by Mt. Rokko. Fukuju is brewed with the finest rice grown in Kyogo and water called Miyamizu that has been chosen as one of the Select Best waters in Japan. Koji (malted rice) is the most important element for the brewing process, that is why Fukuju produces its own Koji by hand in their Koji-muro (a special room where malted rice is cultivated) which has been used for 260 years. We take pride that our sake embodies a crisp and clear taste cultivated from nature's bounty of the ingredients and our traditional hand crafting technique.

福寿のふるさとは、神戸。
六甲山系の美しい自然に囲まれた灘・御影郷。
米は兵庫県育ちの厳選米。
水は日本の名水百選、宮水。
そして清酒の生命「麹」は創業二百六十年来の「箱麹法」による手造りです。
自然の恵みと、人の技が醸し上げた、綺麗でまっすぐな風味が自慢です。

Fukuju 福寿

In the belief that 'great sake comes from great Koji (malted rice) the cultivation of which is the fundamental step in creating excellence', Fukuju produces by hand its Koji, in Koji muro, which has been used for centuries in the brewing process.

Fukuju uses only the best sake rice cultivated by farmers in the northern region of Mt. Rokko, the home of Yamada Nishiki, Japan's finest rice. The sake is brewed with Miyamizu (water from Nishinomiya City), water that has been long valued as ideal for creating excellent sake. Kobe Shu-shin-kan Brewery continues to use traditional handcrafting techniques to lovingly produce sake, with the same careful attention with which children are raised.

PRODUCT NAME: Fukuju Awasaki Sparkling Sake

DESCRIPTION: Fukuju Awasaki is suitable as an aperitif or after-drinking drink. AWASAKI is a sparkling sake produced by inducing the in-bottle secondary fermentation of sake to effect carbonation. Serve chilled, AWASAKI has a sweet yet refreshingly light flavour.

MATCHING DISH: Fukuju's fruity and refreshing flavour suits canapés topped with Pancetta, cottage cheese, caviar, and foie gras.

Fukuju's yeasty aroma goes well with cheeses, such as Grissini Parmesan (Italian bread sticks with parmesan) and Gougère (French, baked savoury choux pastry made of choux dough mixed with cheese).

Fukuju's fragrant aroma and smooth sparkling taste complements traditional and modern quiche dishes.

RICE POLISHING RATIO: 70%

ALCOHOL CONTENT: 6%

皇国晴酒造　株式会社
Mikunihare Shuzo Co., Ltd
296 Ikuji, Kurobe,
TOYAMA 938-0066, Japan
www.mabotaki.co.jp

Mikunihare 皇国晴

Mikunihare was founded in around 1880. Mikunihare has a great water source on their land, which was designated as one of the best waters in Japan by the Ministry of Environment. This water is soft water and it makes for a refreshing and light tasting sake.

Mikunihare is located on the seaside, so our sake goes well with seafood. It goes especially well with white flesh fish, such as king-fish sashimi. The umami taste of the fish and refreshing light taste of our sake create a well-balanced flavour.

You can enjoy our sake chilled in summer and tepid warm (around 45°C) in winter.

皇国晴酒造は1880年ごろ設立された酒蔵で、蔵内に環境省選定・日本名水百選に指定された良質な水が自噴しています。日本名水百選の水が湧き出している酒蔵は日本では当蔵しかありません。
水質は軽やかな軟水ですので、酒質も軽快でさっぱりとしています。皇国晴は海その場にあり、魚介類などとの相性もいいです。特にぶりの刺身がおすすめで、魚のうまみと酒の軽やかさが絶妙に調和しておいしくいただけます。夏は冷やして、冬は45度ぐらいの燗がおすすめです。

=ǁ=ǁ=ǁ=ǁ=ǁ=ǁ=ǁ=ǁ=ǁ=ǁ=ǁ=ǁ=ǁ=ǁ=ǁ=ǁ=ǁ=

PRODUCT NAME:	Maboroshi no taki 幻の瀧　純米吟醸
GRADE:	Dry Junmai-ginjyo
MATCHING DISH:	Masu-zushi is one of the regional cuisines in Toyama. Cured rainbow trout slices in salted vinaigrette sauce and wrapped with sushi rice in a box, and then weighted with stone to form. Masu-zushi is also popular as a local Ekiben (lunch box available at train stations).

皇国晴 MIKUNIHARE

株式会社　宮崎本店
Miyazaki Honten Co., Ltd
972 Minamigomitsuka Kusu-machi
Yokkaiichi City,
MIE 510-0104 Japan
www.miyanoyuki.co.jp

Miyazaki Honten　宮崎本店

Kusu town has always been famous for its abundance of Shochu Breweries. There was more than 30 breweries, but have since been combined into Miyazaki Honten. We at Miyazaki Honten produce a large variety of alcoholic beverages, not only Schou, but also sake, and liquors, even Whisky. Our flag ship shochu, Kinmiya Schochu is very popular in the Izakaya (Japanese tapas style restaurants) of down town Tokyo.

三重県四日市市楠は古くから「灘の清酒、楠の焼酎」と称されるほど酒造りに盛んな地で昔は30以上あった蔵も今ではすべて宮崎本店が請け負って1社のみ。宮崎本店は、日本酒、焼酎、ウイスキー、リキュールとさまざまな種類のお酒を製造しております。
三重県では、「清酒　宮の雪」が伊勢神宮をお膝元に地元ではかなり高い評価を頂いております。ベルギーのモンドセレクションでも、1983年から2013年度まで通算30年連続受賞の偉業を成し遂げ続けております。
また、焼酎のキンミヤ焼酎は東京下町で古くから人気が高く、東京都内の飲食店人気度が抜群に高いです。

=╫=

PRODUCT NAME: KINMIYA SHOCHU　キンミヤ焼酎

DESCRIPTION: Kinmiya Shochu is of the highest quality of Kourui-Shochu, distilled using a continuous stilling method. The usage of local spring water gives it a smooth, slightly sweet and mellow taste. As Kourui-shochu goes well with a large variety of elements, it is popular as a cocktail base, but can also be enjoyed straight.

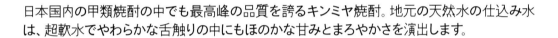

PRODUCT NAME: MIYA NO YUKI　宮の雪

DESCRIPTION: Our sake, Miya No Yuki 'snow in the shrine', has always been a local favourite and has also won gold medals at the Belgium Monde Selections for the past 30 years. It is classified as Genshu, however Miya No Yuki's alcohol level is only 17% vs Genshu 18~20%, which is adjusted by using various techniques, such as fermenting at lower temperatures, using special yeasts, or stopping the fermentation process early. This results in an easy drinking Genshu that still retains a rich and mellow, silky touch.

日本国内の甲類焼酎の中でも最高峰の品質を誇るキンミヤ焼酎。地元の天然水の仕込み水は、超軟水でやわらかな舌触りの中にもほのかな甘みとまろやかさを演出します。

最高級の地元の三重産山田錦を使用し、純粋酵母と手作りの麹を低温でじっくり丁寧に醗酵させてこだわりの純米吟醸です。一般的な加水はせず、そのまま厳守で仕上げてあるため、きれいな舌触りの中にも、しっかりとまろやかな味わいが楽しめます。

Nakajimaya Shuzoujyo 中島屋酒造場
2-1-3 Doi, Shunan city,
YAMAGUCHI 746-0011 Japan
http://y-shuzo.com/hp/nakajimaya.html

Nakajimaya 中島屋

Founded in 1823, our boutique saka-gura brewery is located in Yamaguchi. We use the Kimoto-method (classical sake brewing technique using naturally occurring lactic acid bacteria to propagate naturally) and we are constantly striving to produce ideal sake to match with today's taste.

　Due to the Kimoto-method, our sake creates a distinctive taste with deeper flavour. Its individual acidic fullness and robust flavour lasts longer by warming sake. Our sake can be enjoyed at room temperature as well as warm.

【蔵・商品紹介】
創業1823年、山口の地で小蔵ならではの、きめ細かな手造りを守り続け、現代人の嗜好にマッチする、輝くような存在感あるお酒を、造ることを目指し、酒造りに励みます。
伝統的な製法である生酛で造った本品は、生酛特有の香り、味わいにも、個性豊かな旨みとふくらみのある酸味が調和し、熱燗にも対応する腰の強さが特徴的な辛口のお酒です。
飲み方は、常温〜お燗がお勧めです。

=╫=╫=╫=╫=╫=╫=╫=╫=╫=╫=╫=╫=╫=╫=╫=╫=╫=

PRODUCT NAME: Kimoto Junmai Kanenaka 木元純米　カネタカ

DESCRIPTION: Distinctive taste by Kimoto-method. Rich flavour.
きもとに起因する香り、味わいが個性豊かで、旨みとふくらみのある酸味が熱燗にも対応する腰の強さが特徴。

MATCHING DISHES: **Chishamoni**
This is a simple dish: tear Chisha (a kind of lettuce) into small pieces by hand, and dress with vinaigrette miso. This is a highly nutritious and popular homemade dish in Yamaguchi. Nowadays it is eaten as simple home cooking, but originally it was eaten to entertain guests after the battle of Sekigahara Civil war in 1600 when people were starving without much food.

Kencho
This is a traditional winter dish in Yamaguchi. Sautéed sliced daikon radish and roughly crushed tofu with soy sauce, mirin, sake and sugar. It is also called Kenchou-ni or Kenchou-taki. In some areas people add water to make soup called Kencho-jiru.
　Kencho is usually made in large amounts, once cooled it can be reheated again. The taste becomes mellower than when it is fresh.
　Both dishes have strong umami, so they are well matched with our sake that has a rich taste.

中島屋 NAKAJIMAYA

=〳=〳=〳=〳=〳=〳=〳=〳=〳=〳=〳=〳=〳=〳=〳=〳=

【お酒に合う郷土料理紹介】
ちしゃもみ
関ヶ原の合戦後、防長二国に領地が減った毛利氏の家臣の多くは、食うや食わずの生活をしていました。そんな中冠婚葬祭）や不意の来客のもてなしに出されたのが、「ちしゃなます」でした。生のちしゃを手で適当にちぎり、酢みそであえた簡単な料理ですが、栄養価も高く、最も広く親しまれている山口県の家庭料理です。

けんちょう
けんちょうとは、薄切りの大根と適度な大きさに崩した豆腐を油で炒め、しょう油、みりん、日本酒、砂糖などで味付けして汁気がなくなるまで煮たもので、山口県に伝わる冬の郷土料理です。「けんちょう煮」「けんちょう炊き」とも呼ばれます。けんちょうを汁気の多いまま仕上げて「けんちょう汁」として食べる地域もあります。
大根と豆腐が基本の具材だが、にんじん、油揚げ、里芋、こんにゃく、干し椎茸などを入れる事も多いです。味付けには、だし汁やだしの素を加える事も多く、また、味噌仕立てにする地域もあります。
大鍋で大量に作り、出来上がってしばらくしたもの（作りおきしたもの）を温め直して食べると、味がなじんで美味しくなるとされます。

いずれも、旨みの強い料理で、存在感のある本商品と相性抜群です。

75

男山　株式会社
Otokoyama Co. Ltd
7 Nagayama 2 jo Asahikawa,
HOKKAIDO, Japan
www.otokoyama.com

Otokoyama 男山

The 'Otokoyama' brand of sake originated in Itami, Hyogo Prefecture 340 years ago. Due to financial reasons the company disappeared, until 1899 when it was re-established nationwide. Many companies produce their version of 'Otokoyama' sake, but the brewery Otokoyama Co. Ltd in Asahikawa, Hokkaido is the only one that inherits ties with the original. Since then it has had a loyal following, including many historical notabilities.

The Otokoyama brewery is surrounded by nature in Asahikawa, where the rich underground water originating from the perpetual snow on the Daisetsuzan volcanic group, and severe cold winter are suited for producing sake. It is believed that the water pumped from the underground wells on the premises is a precious water for life longevity.

The Otokoyama brewery has always pursued authentic Japanese sake production methods, carefully polishing the selected sake rice according to the traditional techniques under the superior Toji brewers' rules. Otokoyama has received many awards nationally as well as abroad.

At the Otokoyama sake museum next to the brewery, visitors can find the history of the Otokoyama brewery, including equipment for sake production and also antiques of the Edo era, such as Ukiyoe paintings. In the winter season (usually from November to March in Japan), visitors are able to observe the brewing by brewers through a glass wall. Also tasting and purchasing sake are possible then.

　Otokoyama is presently exported to the USA, across Europe, Australia, and many Asian countries.

男山は寛文年間、今から約340年前に伊丹において醸造を始め、江戸時代から、古今第一の名酒として歴史上に残る有名な方々の愛飲を受け、昔の貴重な資料と共に、現代に伝わる伝統の名酒です。

男山蔵元のある旭川は、大雪山系の万年雪を源とする伏流水と、清酒醸造に最も適した厳しい寒さの気候風土に恵まれております。この地で、全国より酒造好適米を選りすぐり、高精白に磨いた原料米を使用し、歴史と伝統の技をもとに、常に本物を求め、酒造りに励んでおります。品質の面では、国内はもとより海外の酒類コンクールにおいて数々の金賞受賞に輝いております。

併設してある「男山酒造り資料館」は、3階に昔の酒造り道具が、2階には浮世絵を中心とした江戸時代の資料室や海外の酒類コンクールで受賞したメダル・賞状などが数多く展示されています。加えて、冬季の仕込みの時期であれば、ガラス越しに酒造りの作業の様子を見ることができます。1階には、試飲・販売ができるコーナーに、季節限定や蔵元限定の日本酒があります。

蔵元で地下より汲み上げている男山の仕込み水伏流水は、「延命長寿の水」として市民に親しまれ、毎日多くの人が汲みに来ています。

アメリカには１９８４年、オーストラリアには１９９０年より輸出しています。
男山酒造り資料館には年間約１２万人のお客様が来館して、海外からも４万人ほど来ている。

PRODUCT NAME: Otokoyama Junmai Daiginjo　男山純米大吟醸（純米大吟醸）

DESCRIPTION: When you sip the sake, a soft aroma envelopes the nose. This sake is clean and dry, yet has an elegance and depth of richness. Recommended serving temperature: Chilled

RICE POLISHING RATIO: 38%

ALCOHOL CONTENT: 16%

=╫=╫=╫=╫=╫=╫=╫=╫=╫=╫=╫=╫=╫=╫=╫=╫=╫=╫=

PRODUCT NAME: Otokoyama Yushutsu Junmai　男山輸出純米（特別純米）

DESCRIPTION: This is limited brewed sake for the overseas market. It is a rich but mellow dry sake that can be enjoyed often without losing its charm.

SERVING: Chilled or room temperature

=╫=╫=╫=╫=╫=╫=╫=╫=╫=╫=╫=╫=╫=╫=╫=╫=╫=╫=

PRODUCT NAME: Otokoyama Kimoto-method Junmai　男山キモト純米（純米）

DESCRIPTION: Kimoto is a labor intensive and traditional method of making the yeast starter. It tends to give a deep aroma, which is not only suitable for the chilled style but also for the warmer sake. We brew this superior quality sake with our original yeast.

SERVING: Chilled, room temperature or lukewarm (around 30°C)
蔵独特の酵母を育成して醸造したキモト造りの芳醇な辛口
飲み方のおすすめ　冷やして・常温・ぬる燗

FOOD: We believe that sake goes well with all Japanese food, but especially those from Hokkaido, such as 'grilled fish', 'scallop Sashimi', hot dishes, etc.

日本酒は日本食全般に相性が良いという考えを持っていますので特にお勧めすることは致しません。
ただ、地（北海道）の料理に合うということは自信を持って言えます。

例　焼き魚（ほっけ、にしん、さんま、・・・・）
　　刺身（白身魚・ホタテなど貝類・・・）
　　ジンギスカン鍋・三平汁など

=╫=╫=╫=╫=╫=╫=╫=╫=╫=╫=╫=╫=╫=╫=╫=╫=╫=╫=

薩摩酒造　株式会社
Satsuma Shuzo Co., Ltd
26 Tategamihonmachi Makurazaki-city,
Kagoshima 898-0025, Japan
Tel: +81-993-72-1231 Fax: +81-993-73-1886
http://www.satsuma.co.jp/english/index.html

Satsuma 薩摩

Satsuma Shuzo is one of the most famous 'shochu' makers in Japan. 'Shochu' is a Japanese traditional hard liquor, distilled spirits made from grains and vegetables. The most common base ingredients are sweet potato, barley, rice, buckwheat and sugar cane. Japanese Honkaku Shochu (traditional premium shochu) is made by single distillation unlike other hard liquors as vodka. It is distilled only once in its whole manufacturing process so it retains enjoyable natural flavour of its main ingredients and that is why it is considered as the premium. The master brewer's skill, quality ingredients and good water are necessary to make good shochu. Our company policy is 'quality first', we are producing shochu with care in accordance with this policy.

=╟=╟=╟=╟=╟=╟=╟=╟=╟=╟=╟=╟=╟=╟=╟=

PRODUCT NAME:	SATSUMA SHIRANAMI
TYPE:	Imo Shochu (Distilled spirits made from sweet potato)
ALCOHOL CONTENT:	25% (50Proof)
KOJI (MALT STARTER):	Shiro Koji (White Koji)
DISTILLATION METHOD:	Normal pressure, Single Distillation
DESCRIPTION:	Shiranami is one of the most popular sweet potato shochu brands in Japan. It has established its high reputation and brand name in the Japanese market for a long period of time. We use select Kogane sengan sweet potato from south Kagoshima, Japan and our highly skilled shochu master distiller (Toji) prepare this shochu with care and his special technique. It has the natural sweetness of the sweet potato and an excellent sweet potato aroma with body.

=⫻=⫻=⫻=⫻=⫻=⫻=⫻=⫻=⫻=⫻=⫻=⫻=⫻=⫻=⫻=⫻=⫻=

PRODUCT NAME:	KURO SHIRANAMI
TYPE:	Imo Shochu (Distilled spirits made from sweet potato)
ALCOHOL CONTENT:	25%(50 Proof)
KOJI (MALT STARTER):	Kuro Koji (Black Koji)
DISTILLATION METHOD:	Normal pressure, single Distillation
DESCRIPTION:	Kuro Shiranami is made from select Kogane Sengan Sweet potato from south Kasoshima. It is prepared with Black Koji so it has mild sweetness and an excellent aroma with a smooth finish. Kuro shiranami won the highest award in the 2012 Kagoshima Honkaku Shochu competition which 110+ distilleries (244 shochu brands) participated in.

=⫻=⫻=⫻=⫻=⫻=⫻=⫻=⫻=⫻=⫻=⫻=⫻=⫻=⫻=⫻=⫻=⫻=

PRODUCT NAME:	KANNOKO
TYPE:	Mugi Shochu (Distilled spirits made from Barley)
ALCOHOL CONTENT:	25%(50 Proof)
KOJI (MALT STARTER):	Shiro Koji (White Koji)
DISTILLATION METHOD:	Normal pressure, single Distillation
DESCRIPTION:	This shochu is made from 100% select barley. It is aged deliberately in oak barrels over 3 years for its mellow yet smooth taste with a light smoky oak aroma. It is one of the best-selling aged barley shochu in Japan. We own our cooperage in Kagoshima and our cooper maintains our barrels to continue producing the best quality barrel aged shochu.

=⫻=⫻=⫻=⫻=⫻=⫻=⫻=⫻=⫻=⫻=⫻=⫻=⫻=⫻=⫻=⫻=⫻=

関原酒造　株式会社
Sekihara Shuzo Co., Ltd
1-1029-1 Sekihara-cho Nagaoka city
NIIGATA 940-2035 Japan
www.sake-sekihara.com

Sekihara 関原

Since establishment in 1716, Sekihara Shuzo has continuously produced sake regardless of war or natural disaster. Niigata is one of the most well-known rice and sake producing regions. Sekihara's sake is produced using Niigata's best sake rice and soft pure snow water using traditional methods. We cherish the fact we have been bringing out the flavour of sake rice for 300 years.

　江戸時代中期、享保元年 (1716) の創業以来およそ300年、一冬も休むことなく酒造り一筋に魂を注いできました。連綿と受け継がれた伝統の寒造りの技で醸す日本酒は悠久の大河、信濃川の伏流水と日本有数の米どころ新潟の米の良さを余すことなく引き出した逸品揃いです。

=╞╡=╞╡=╞╡=╞╡=╞╡=╞╡=╞╡=╞╡=╞╡=╞╡=╞╡=╞╡=╞╡=╞╡=

PRODUCT NAME: Echigo NAGAOKA-HAN Tokubetsu Junmai-shu
越後長岡藩　特別純米酒

DESCRIPTION: In the rigorous Niigata winter, specially selected sake rice is polished (60% rice polishing ratio) and elaborately fermented to produce our flagship sake, 'Echigo Nagaoka-han'. It is a slightly dry and rich flavoured sake.

It goes well with seafood, such as sashimi and 'Nina', one of the regional stewed dishes in Niigata. Enjoy cold or warm.

厳選した原料米は60%まで磨き上げ雪深い新潟の厳冬期、丹念に仕込まれ「越後長岡藩　特別純米酒」となります。やや辛口でコクを感じる特別純米酒は刺身などの魚料理や煮菜など新潟の郷土料理との相性が抜群で冷やしてキレの良さを、温めてまろやかさをお楽しみいただけます。

MATCHING DISH: **Nina**

One of the popular regional cuisines in Niigata. Harvested Taina (Chinese mustard leaves) or Nozawana-green vegetable in autumn and pickled in salt for a preserved food for winter. Nina is a simple home style cooking dish using these pickled Taina or Nozawana, stir-fried with other ingredients.

煮菜（にな）

新潟を代表する郷土料理「煮菜（にな）」は秋に収穫した体菜（たいな）や野沢菜、小松菜などを塩漬けにして保存し冬に取り出し、塩出しして打豆、油揚などと煮て作る新潟の昔ながらの一品です。

=╫=╫=╫=╫=╫=╫=╫=╫=╫=╫=╫=╫=╫=╫=╫=╫=╫=╫=╫=

須藤本家　株式会社 Sudohonke Inc
2215 Obara, Kasama
IBARAKI 309-1701 Japan
www.sudohonke.co.jp

Sudohonke 須藤本家

The exact founded year is unknown, but according to the oldest record it is said that Sudo Honke had already started brewing sake in 1141. It is the oldest sake brewery in Japan and is known as the first brewery to produce 'unpasteurized sake' 生酒 Nama-zake.

'Our brewery is located in a place called Obara, which is about a ten minute drive from Tomobe Station, and one hour from Tokyo by the JR Joban Line's Super Hitachi train.

Obara is one of the original settlements of the Ibaraki Prefecture. Even today, the remains of the embankment of a castle from the Heian Era remain in the area. The local people often refer to us as "that brewery in the grove," surrounded as we are by lush keyaki (zelkova) trees.

The way our brewery came into existence is a bit different from other breweries. Originally we were members of the warrior class, and sake brewing began after the economy came to be based on rice, and local economies stabilized. Sake brewing was a by-product of the main product, rice. For this reason, there were two names associated with our family: Buza Emon was the warrior name, and Gen Uemon for the sake-brewing name.'

Yoshiyasu Sudo, 55th Generation President

Sudo Honke brews sake with the utilization of natural resources; drawing underground water from three wells in the brewery, cultivating rice fields with fully ripened compost.

　酒蔵は東京から北に80km、茨城県の真ん中、県名発祥の地の一つ、笠間市小原にあります。古墳が多く、戦国期以前の土塁がそのまま敷地内に残っています。酒蔵を守る様に古木が鬱蒼と茂り、愛称は「杜の蔵」。おろし風が厳しい寒の精霊な空気と水の時に醸します。仕込水は蔵内3カ所の井戸の豊かな伏流水。

醸すのは純米吟醸と純米大吟醸のみです。日本で初めて「生」の酒を出した酒蔵で、家訓は「にごり」と「生もと」を絶やすな、活性にごりは数百年来スパークリングです。熟成酒は1973 (昭和48) 年のヴィンテージから暦年「生」で蔵出し中です。パーカーズ・ポイントは91点。International Wine Challenge では各賞を受賞しています。

須藤源右衛門

Kakunko　花薫光
Junmai Daiginjo-shu, unfiltered and unpasteurized. It has a highly distinctive rich fragrance with a silky smooth texture.

Flagship Nama-zake, Kakunko has won International Wine Challenges and was given 91/100 points by Robert M. Parker (wine critic).

Sato no Homare 郷乃誉
Junmai ginjo-shu. Unfiltered. Pasteurized.

Hana awase 花あわせ
Junmai Ginjo-shu. Unfiltered. Unpasteurized

Yuzura 山桜桃
Junmai Ginjo-shu. Unfiltered Unpasteurized

Taiwakura Shuzo Co., Ltd. 大和蔵酒造 株式会社
8-1 Matsusakadaira, Taiwa-cho, Kurokawa-gun
MIYAGI 981-3408 Japan
www.miyagisake.jp

Taiwakura 大和蔵

Taiwakura Shuzo is a new brewery re-established in 1996 from Yamagata. Taiwakura is located in the central part of Miyagi Prefecture, Taiwa town, Kurokawa district. It is known as the production area of 'Miyagi Rice', one of the most popular in Japan, and is blessed with the fresh and clean water from the Funagata Mountains.

Since its inception, Taiwakura has challenged the sake brewing by merging the traditional skills of 'Nanbu Toji', the sake master from Iwate Prefecture, and modern production facilities. Taiwakura developed a collaboration between brewing with the latest equipment and the traditional hand-made brewing to produce a superior sake. In 2006 'Yuki no Matsushima' brand was succeeded by Miyagi-Shurui. Taiwakura continues to brew the sake with passion, pursuing the ideal sake, which has a rich in rice flavour and crisp finish.

Taiwakura produces their sake with soft water by slow fermentation. Toji traditional sake brewing methods combined with modern technology are used to bring out the character of sake rice. Junmai-shu, Ginjyo-shu, and super dry sake have their own individual characteristics, which are enjoyed by many sake fans.

会社案内
蔵の歴史・銘柄の由来
大和蔵の前身は、山形県高畠町で、寛政十年創業以来、百八十余年の伝統と歴史を持つ老舗の蔵でした。現在の宮城県大和町に移転したのは平成8年のこと。この移転を機に、醸造所の商号を、地名にちなんで「大和蔵酒造株式会社」と改め、近代的な日本酒醸造プラントを建設しました。

平成18年には宮城酒類㈱様より「雪の松島」ブランドを譲り受けたのを期に、更に酒質の高上を目指すべく、最新の設備と手造りを融合した酒造りに取り組んでおります。

蔵の方針

仕込み水は軟水で長期発酵タイプ。南部杜氏の伝統技術を現代的な感覚で生かし、出来る限り米の持ち味をうまく引き出すことを重点に醸造されています。純米酒・吟醸酒・とびっきり辛い酒（超辛）など、それぞれに特色があり、その旨味は清酒党に根強い人気をいただいております。

=〃=〃=〃=〃=〃=〃=〃=〃=〃=〃=〃=〃=〃=〃=〃=〃=

PRODUCT NAME: Yuki-no Matsushima Tokubetsu Junmai-shu
雪の松島　特別純米酒

DESCRIPTION: This sake has a soft aroma and rich flavour with Umami. A well-finished and yet an enjoyable aftertaste that invites a second sip without hesitation.

SERVING: Chilled, room temperature or lukewarm

MATCHING DISHES: Sushi, Hiyayakko (Silken tofu salad), Chicken Yakitori, pot dishes, fish cakes, etc

穏やかな香りとふくらみのある味わいが純米酒らしいしっかりとした旨味を際立たせます。キレとともに余韻が残り、また口にしたくなる不思議な酒です。

お勧めの飲み方：冷・常温・ぬる燗とさまざま温度帯で楽しめます。

相性のよい料理：寿司・焼き鳥・冷ややっこ・各種鍋物・かまぼこ等

=〃=〃=〃=〃=〃=〃=〃=〃=〃=〃=〃=〃=〃=〃=〃=〃=

PRODUCT NAME: Yuki-no Matsushima Junmai-shu
雪の松島　純米酒

DESCRIPTION: Rich in taste and super dry finish. Sweet aroma of rice on the nose, texture is gentle and elegant Umami-taste spread on your tongue.

SERVING: Chilled or on the rocks

MATCHING DISHES: Sashimi, Hiyayakko (Silken tofu salad), marinade salad, oily dishes

超辛口の酒でおなじみの「雪の松島」が従来の酒質とは対照的な極甘口の純米酒を造りました。

米の甘みを感じる上立ち香もほんのりとあり、奇麗な旨みが滑らかに喉をつたう優しい口当たりの酒です。

お勧めの飲み方：オンザロックでも美味しくいただけます。

相性のよい料理：冷奴・各種おひたし・他（そば飯・ポテトコロッケ）等、油分が効いた料理にも良く合います。

=〃=〃=〃=〃=〃=〃=〃=〃=〃=〃=〃=〃=〃=〃=〃=〃=

Regional cuisine in Miyagi

Sasa-kama boko: One of fish products. Bamboo leave shaped fish cake.

Gyu-tan: dishes using beef tongue. This dish is the most well known dish in Sendai-city.

玉乃光酒造　株式会社
Tamanohikari Sake Brewing Co., Ltd
545 Higashisakai Machi Fushimi-ku
KYOTO 612-8066 Japan
www.tamanohikari.co.jp

Tamanohikari　玉乃光

For over 330 years since its foundation in 1673 at the first year of the Enpou age of the Edo era by our founder Rokuzaemon Nakaya, Tamanohikari has constantly been striving to manufacture excellent Japanese sake. Owing to the rice shortage during and after the Second World War, the addition of an increased amount of alcohol was formed as a national policy. In the year 1964, for the first time in the history of the industries, Tamanohikari developed an 'Additive free sake' known today as Junmai-shu, which did not contain any alcohol, glucose or preservatives. In the year 1980, we upgraded all the Junmai-shu by using the Ginjo System. Under the principle of *'Good sake is brewed from good brewer's rice'*, we have dedicated our efforts since then, to produce better brewer's rice in conjunction with farmers and contract farmers from every production area. Our yield is approximately 5000 koku (unit for measuring a yield of crop, 1-koku=180l) of rice.

初代、中村屋六座衛門が延宝元年 (1673年) に創業して以来330年余、玉乃光は常に優れた日本酒造りに努めてまいりました。戦中、戦後のコメ不足を理由に、昭和19年より、増量用アルコールの添加が国策となっていました。昭和39年玉乃光は業界に先駆けてアルコール、ブドウ糖だけでなく防腐剤をいれない「無添加清酒」(今日の純米酒) を開発。昭和55年には純米酒をすべて吟醸造りにレベルアップしました。以降、「よい酒造りはよい酒米から」との信念の下、各産地の農家との契約的な栽培により、酒米つくりに取り組んでいます。石高は現在約5000石。

We at Tamanohikari, have continued to brew high quality handmade sake for 340 years since we were first established. Our sake is not fancy or trendy, but instead we have aimed to create a classic liquor which would be the best complement for your meals.

In order to achieve our goal, Mr. Morimoto, the master brewer and his brewers come over to make sake every year from Tajima Hyogo Prefecture. They have made the taste of Tamanohikari. Their spirit creates this natural fruity flavour. We believe that the master brewer puts two important messages into his work. The first is that the raw materials rice, yeast, plant and yeast fungus are natural creatures.

He believes that it is important to keep the creature in a better condition to live through interacting with them. Therefore brewers are always required to take care with the changes of conditions carefully during their routine work.

The second is 'harmony and reliability' among brewers. In the sake brewing process, each brewer is responsible for a different part. They are required to get detailed information from the previous process, which is very difficult to measure, and then they have to pass this subtle information to the next brewers. The main information is noted in numerical values measured by chemical analysis, but this detailed information cannot be conveyed unless there is harmony in the relationship.

Good sake is never made without good human relationships among brewers. The master brewer believes that keeping a good relationship is the most important step of sake making. Only after practicing these two points, can we serve the high quality sake to you. 'Rice, water, koji and human spirit.'

These are the keywords of Tamanohikari Sake Brewery and the Master Brewer, Mr Morimoto.

玉乃光酒造は、創業以来340年、まじめによい酒をとの思いから手作りで酒造りを続けています。派手なおさけでも、今風の流行のお酒でもない、飽きのこない食事を引き立てる酒を目指しています。
この思いを成就するため、毎年、酒造りには兵庫県但馬から、森本杜氏と数人の蔵人を招き、彼らのよい酒を生み出す心意気が玉乃光の味を造っています。その重要な2つのポイントとは、第一に「原料：米、麹菌、酵母菌は自然界の生き物であるということ」。第二に「人の和のつながり」です。すなわち、酒造りは原料となる生き物と仲良く対話し、自然界の生き物の求めに応じてその生活環境をよりよい状態に保つことがよい酒造りにおいて重要であり、蔵人は常に生き物の状態に気を配りその変化に対応していくことが不可欠です。また酒造りは蔵人がそれぞれの部分を担当し行いますが、自分の担当する前工程における数値では表せない微妙な情報を把握する必要があります。また、後の工程においても同様に情報を伝達しなければなりません。主な情報は分析値などの数値で伝達されますが、このような微妙な情報は人

間関係が円満であってはじめて伝わるものです。ぎくしゃくした人間関係の中では決してよい
酒は生み出せません。杜氏はこの点を考慮し、蔵人の「和」をいかに保つかが酒造りの最重要
課題と考えています。

「米、水、麹、心意気。ただよい酒を３４０年」

═╟═╟═╟═╟═╟═╟═╟═╟═╟═╟═╟═╟═╟═╟═╟═╟═╟═╟═╟═

PRODUCT NAME: Tamanohikari Junmai Daiginjo　玉乃光　純米大吟醸

DESCRIPTION: Tamanohikari Shuzo presents its junmai daiginjo sake, using only the rarest Bizen Omachi rice. Natural acidity and umami from the rice yield and exquisitely balanced sake. The flavour glides silky smooth over the palate with a crisp, refreshing finish.

RICE: 100 % Bizen-omachi rice　備前雄町米１００％

SERVING: Chilled

MATCHING DISHES: Sashimi, Grilled duck with Japanese sansho pepper.
　　Tamanohikari is on the dry side and is a well finished sake, so it cleanses your palate, and brings out the taste of sashimi. Not only that, this sake has a fruity aroma and rich umami as well. These elements match the umami of duck.
和食の定番であるお刺身と酒米の元祖である備前雄町米を使った純米大吟醸とのペアリング。辛口ですっきりとしたお酒の味わいがお刺身のうまみを引き立ててくれます。京料理の名物、鴨を使った山椒焼き、鴨をじっくり焼いたうまみとお酒との相性は抜群。

═╟═╟═╟═╟═╟═╟═╟═╟═╟═╟═╟═╟═╟═╟═╟═╟═╟═╟═╟═

PRODUCT NAME: Tamanohikari Yamahai Junmai ginjo　玉乃光　山廃

DESCRIPTION: Brewing by a traditional brewing method called 'Yamaoroshihaishimoto', its method produces pure sake without fortifying it with alcohol or additives, using 60% milled sake-making rice with natural yeasts and lactobacilli from our 100 year old brewery. It takes twice as long to produce this sake, which reflects the extra care we take. The full-bodied taste gives a distinctive impact like Bourbon Whisky.

SERVING: Tepid warm.
初夏の味覚京都の筍、近江牛を使ったお鍋。味わい的には濃い口ということもあり、手間ひまかけて作った山廃が味を引き立ててくれます。特に寒い冬の時期はお燗酒、もしくはぬる燗でおいしく召し上がれます。

═╟═╟═╟═╟═╟═╟═╟═╟═╟═╟═╟═╟═╟═╟═╟═╟═╟═╟═╟═

樽平酒造　株式会社
Taruhei Brewing Co., Ltd
2886 Nakakomatsu Kawanishimachi (Oaza) Higashiokitama-gun
YAMAGATA 999-0122
www.taruhei.co.jp

Taruhei　樽平

To pursue 'the real sake' using the traditional sake brewing methods, we aim to brew Junmai-Karakuchi taruzake (dry junmai-shu in cask sake) to the highest quality. To brew our dry and tasty sake we take particular care to use only the finest raw materials. We then take care at every stage in our brewing process ensuring that our sake is the finest quality, unique and that you will never become weary of drinking it.

Established in 1695. We have more than 300-years history of sake brewing. The current head is the 12th generation. In 1995, our brewery was shown in the drama 'Kura' (author: Ms. Tomiko Miyao) broadcasted by NHK television Network, the drama portrayed life from 1905 and reproduced the traditional hand brewing method. Our famous sake 'Sumiyoshi' was also featured in 'Oishinbo' (comic book written by Mr. Tetsu Kariya).

昔ながらの伝統的な製法により、「本物の日本酒」を製造販売し、他メーカーのまねのできない品質本位の純米辛口樽酒で、原料のみならず総てにこだわり、辛口であり、辛く感じさせない旨口の酒、飲み飽きしない飲みごたえのする独特の個性ある本物の日本酒づくりを標にしております。
　創業は元禄年間（１６９５年頃）で３００余年の伝統を誇り、現社長は十二代目である。平成7年、宮尾登美子原作の「蔵」の収録（NHKドラマ）が、明治38年頃の時代背景と昔ながらの手

づくりの酒造りを再現出来るとして弊社で行われた。また、雁屋哲氏の名作「美味しんぼ」に弊社の人気ブランド「住吉」が紹介され、多くの愛飲家に好評をいただいております。

　弊社では、活性炭による濾過をおこなっていないため、お酒本来の色「山吹色」を呈しております。

Since we use activated carbon to filter without using colour adjustment our sake has a bright yellow colour.

═〴═〴═〴═〴═〴═〴═〴═〴═〴═〴═〴═〴═〴═〴═〴═〴═〴═〴═

PRODUCT NAME:	Kin Sumiyoshi Tokubetsu Junmai shu金住吉　特別純米酒
DESCRIPTION:	Slowly fermented in barrels, this is a full, dry sake with umami taste of rice.
POLISHED RATIO:	60%.
ALCOHOL CONTENT:	15.1 %
SERVING:	lukewarm like body temperature or room temperature

═〴═〴═〴═〴═〴═〴═〴═〴═〴═〴═〴═〴═〴═〴═〴═〴═〴═〴═

PRODUCT NAME:	Taruhei　樽平
DESCRIPTION:	This sake is not as dry as Sumiyoshi. Slowly fermented in barrels. A profoundly enjoyable Japanese sake.
POLISHED RATIO:	60 %
ALCOHOL CONTENT:	18.5%
SERVING:	lukewarm like body temperature or room temperature. Keep the sake in the dark cool area or refrigerate.

═〴═〴═〴═〴═〴═〴═〴═〴═〴═〴═〴═〴═〴═〴═〴═〴═〴═〴═

MATCHING DISHES:	Since our sake are mature, they go very well with rich flavour dishes. 'Imo-ni' using Yonezawa-gyu: a stewed dish, stewed satomimo (Mountain potato) with varieties of vegetables and wagyu beef raised in Yonezawa region in sake and soy sauce. 熟成タイプのお酒ですので、和・洋・中、いずれも濃厚な味わいのお料理を

①　いも煮
米沢牛肉は血統と丁寧な飼育、米沢地方の気候が育てる
天然飼料で家族同然に育てられ天塩にかけた米沢牛のうまさと
新鮮な野菜・里芋・こんにゃく・きのこを、酒、しょうゆで一緒に煮込んだ「いも煮」は
深い味わいがあって、酒飲みには酒との相性も抜群で、ついつい
飲みすぎる状態で大変にお客様に喜ばれている山形名物です。

═〴═〴═〴═〴═〴═〴═〴═〴═〴═〴═〴═〴═〴═〴═〴═〴═〴═〴═

司牡丹酒造　株式会社
Tsukasabotan Sake Brewing Co., Ltd
1299 Ko, Sakawa, Takaoka cho,
KOCHI 789-1201, Japan
+81 889-22-1211
www.tsukasabotan.co.jp

Tsukasabotan 司牡丹

Our antecedents' brewery was established in Sakawa, Kochi Prefecture in 1603. The brewery was approved to visit and sell to Samurai residences, which was a great honour. Since then, the traditional sake brewing method has been handed down from one generation to the next. In 1918 sake breweries in Sagawa town were combined as a modern stock corporation.

We have produced sake with quality 'Yamada-nishiki' sake rice mainly from Hyogo where it is famous for producing sake rice, at the same time we have made an effort to produce organic local sake rice in Kochi. The source of water is from the spring water coming from the Niyodo River which is known as the clearest river in Japan.

'Wa 和' is one of Tsukasabotan's mottos: It literally means 'harmony'. Producing sake involves 'harmony among Japanese tradition, culture and spirit', 'balancing between skills/technology and nature', 'balancing aroma and flavour to match with foods'. Our goal is to help to make smooth relationships in society and for people to live in harmony.

=╫=╫=╫=╫=╫=╫=╫=╫=╫=╫=╫=╫=╫=╫=╫=╫=╫=╫=

PRODUCT NAME:	Senchu hassaku Tokubetsu Junmai　船中八策　特別純米
DESCRIPTION:	Extra dry and well-finished sake, yet a smooth and rich flavour blossom in your mouth.
RICE:	Yamadanishiki / Matsuyamamitsui
POLISHING RATIO:	60%
ALCOHOL CONTENT:	15–16%
SERVING:	8–10°C
MATCHING DISHES:	Seared or Sashimi Bonito Grilled gill of yellowtail White fish Tempura

超辛口でありながらきわめて滑らかに味わいが口中で膨らみ、後味はスッキリとしている。
カツオのタタキ。カツオの刺身、カツオかま塩焼き、白身魚の天ぷら。

=//=

PRODUCT NAME: Ware tada taru wo shiru　吾唯足知　純米吟醸

DESCRIPTION: This sake has an elegant and delicate aroma, the texture is smooth with soft Umami and refreshing acidity are balanced and spread across your tongue.

RICE: Yamadanishiki

POLISHING RATIO: 60%

ALCOHOL CONTENT: 15-16%

SERVING: 8–10°C

MATCHING DISHES: Tempura, sake steamed snapper
優雅で繊細な吟醸香を持ち、滑らかでソフトな旨味とフレッシュな酸味が調和しながら口中で広がっていく
てんぷら,真鯛の酒蒸し

=//=

PRODUCT NAME: Yama Yuzu shibori yuzu no sake (citrus sake)　山柚子搾りゆずの酒

DESCRIPTION: This sake is a fruit based liquor. It has added fresh citron juice and has elegant sweetness. There are no additives contained. Aperitif or digestif. It is recommended to be chilled and enjoyed with ice, straight, or with soda water.

ALCOHOL CONTENT: 8%

SERVING: 8-10°C
柚子の生果汁をそのまま味わうような感覚で楽しめます。とにかくフレッシュで、甘さも上品です。冷蔵庫で冷やしてお飲み下さい。香料・着色料・酸味料・保存料などは一切無添加。日本酒ベースで低アルコール、かつ本当に美味しいリキュール
食前酒や食後酒、オンザロック、ストレート(冷やして8℃〜10℃)、ソーダ割り

=//=

<司牡丹の由来>

　南国土佐、高知市を離れて西へ26ｋｍ、山紫水明の佐川町は銘酒「司牡丹」醸造の地として名があります。今から約400余年の昔、関ヶ原の合戦直後の慶長8年（1603年）のことです。関ヶ原の勲功により、徳川家康から土佐24万石を賜った山内一豊に伴い、土佐に入国した山内家の首席家老、深尾和泉守重良は佐川1万石を預かることになります。その時、深尾氏に従ってきた商家の中には、酒造りを業とする「御酒屋」の名が見られました。深尾家出入りの御用商人で「名字・帯刀」を許された格式ある酒屋です。この酒屋が、司牡丹酒造の前身であります。以来、佐川の地に伝統正しい酒造りが受け継がれ、大正7年（1918年）、佐川の酒造家が結集して近代企業として株式会社を設立。そして佐川出身の維新の志士、明治新政府の宮内大臣も務めた田中光顕伯爵（坂本龍馬、中岡慎太郎亡き後の陸援隊長）は、この佐川の酒を愛飲し、「天下の芳醇なり、今後は酒の王たるべし」と激励の一筆を寄せ「司牡丹」と命名。「牡丹は百花の王、さらに牡丹の中の司たるべし」という意味であります。

<社宝「芳醇無比乃巻」>

　昭和5年（1930年）、高知県出身で時の総理大臣、浜口雄幸首相から司牡丹に「芳醇無比」の賛辞の一筆が届けられました。これを聞いた司牡丹の名付け親、田中光顕伯爵は「私も何か言葉を添えよう」と一筆をしたため、「空谷と名にはよべども水音も跫音も高く世にとどきけり」「酒の名の牡丹は獅子によりてこそ高くかほらめ千代の世までも」の二首を寄せられます。これは、浜口首相の一筆と合わせて表装の上「芳醇無比乃巻」と箱書きまでされた丁重な贈答でありました。「空谷」は浜口首相の雅号から、「獅子」はライオン宰相の異名から、そして百花の王「牡丹」は百獣の王「獅子」とは切っても切れぬ関係。つまり、「ライオン宰相浜口雄幸の名声と共に、司牡丹はいつまでも酒の王者であろう」という意味なのです。その後、田中泊より手紙が届き、「ずっと気になっていたが、やはり下の七字の＜千代の世までも＞は＜のちの世までも＞の方が良いと佐々木信綱博士にも言われたので書き直したい。面倒だが送り返してほしい。」とのこと。間もなく、改めて書き直されたものが再び表装されて届けられました。
「酒の名の牡丹は獅子によりてこそ　高くかほらめ　のちの世までも」
これが、現在も社宝として司牡丹酒造に所蔵されている「芳醇無比乃巻」なのです。

『司牡丹酒造の社是：「源・和・創・献」』

「源」：目標に向かって邁進することは大切ですが、意識が外にのみ向いてしまいがちになる危険があります。私たちは、目標に向かって邁進しながらも、しっかりと地に足をつけ、「源」とつながりを持ち続けます。「源」とつながるとは、自分の根源とつながることであり、400年を越える司牡丹の歴史における竹村源十郎を筆頭とする先人たちの心とつながることであり、坂本龍馬を筆頭とする幾多の土佐の偉人たちの心とつながることであり、世界の叡智の源とつながることです。私たちは、彼らに対して恥じるような行い、卑しい行いは断じてしません。私たちは皆、竹村源十郎の心の子孫であり、坂本龍馬の心の子孫です。常にそのことを念頭におき、背筋を凛と伸ばして生きてゆきます。

「和」：私たちは以下の4つの「和」を大切にします。日本古来の伝統・文化・精神の結晶が日本酒であるという意識を持ち（ジャパニーズの「和」）、技術と自然のバランス、蔵元と社員・蔵人とのバランスを大切に（バランスの「和」）、香りと味わいの絶妙な調和を持ち、料理とも調和する日本酒を、調和をもって醸造し、調和をもって製品化、調和をもって販売する（ハーモニーの「和」）。そしてその酒が多くの人間関係において潤滑油となり、世の人々が素晴らしい大調和の中に生活できることを念願とする（コミュニケーションの「和」）。

「創」：ビジネスとは需要を創造することです。世の中で私たちにしか思いつくことができない価値の伝え方を発見し、お客様に語りかけなければ、生まれなかった需要というものがあるのです。私たちは日々需要の創造に精進します。そしてその創造の力を、他のあらゆる業務においても発揮します。

「献」：私たちは、様々な企業活動を通じて、地域や社会に対して貢献します。また企業活動以外に一人の土佐人、一人の日本人としても、悦びに満ちたあたたかい社会を築くため、具体的な地域貢献・社会貢献活動に積極的に取り組みます。

＜司牡丹酒造のミッション（使命）＞
「土佐」「本物」「エコロジー」にこだわった美味しい日本酒を製造販売し、
人々にワクワクするような日本酒の愉しさを伝道する。
その結果、個人には元気と健康と幸せを、
社会には潤滑で円満な人間関係をもたらし、世の中に進歩と調和をもたらす。

株式会社　佐浦 Saura Co., Ltd
2-19 Motomachi, Shiogama, Miyagi,
985-0052 JAPAN
+81-22-362-4165
http://www.urakasumi.com/
info@urakasumi.com

Urakasumi 浦霞

The name of our sake 'Urakasumi', means 'Misty Bay' (*Ura* is Bay and *Kasumi* is Mist). The main brewery is located in Shiogama, a place of scenic beauty facing the Pacific Ocean. 'Urakasumi' comes from an ancient poem which extols the scenery of Shiogama. The poem is about the joy of the arrival of spring and its peaceful scenery at Shiogama Bay. The quality of Urakasumi's sake is well-matched with the image of Misty Bay.

Characteristics of Our Sake ~ Classic and Elegant ~

Urakasumi's sake has been appreciated as 'classic and elegant' sake by consumers. It offers you the true, classic taste of sake. The flavour and aroma are well balanced, and it has a mild and elegant mouth-feel. We are certain that Urakasumi sake will provide you with a peaceful and pleasant time.

Expression of Rationality

We are particular about including regional characteristics in our sake. We primarily use rice produced in Miyagi, one of the premier rice growing areas in Japan. In addition, making a sake that goes well with our regional culinary culture is of another importance. Urakasumi goes especially well with fresh oysters and tuna.

Pursuing the Highest Quality

The honorary Toji (a master sake brewer) Juichi Hirano has underpinned Urakasumi's sake brewing for more than half a century. He has won numerous awards and is well known as one of the best master sake brewers in Japan.

To achieve the best possible standard, these are some of our unique features:

For Daiginjo-shu (super-premium sake), we use Yamadanishiki, the highest quality sake rice, and finely polished rice is fermented at low temperatures over a long period with our house yeast.

- Our house yeast was registered as Kyokai No.12 by the Brewing society of Japan in 1986 for having superior quality Ginjo (premium) flavour.
- Having received many awards in contests held by the National Research Institute of Brewing, we are ranked as a top-level brewery in Japan.
- With detailed management and analysis, we are continuously improving the quality of our sake.

=//=//=//=//=//=//=//=//=//=//=//=//=//=//=//=//=//=

PRODUCT NAME: Urakasumi Yamada Nishiki Junmai-daiginjo
浦霞　山田錦　純米大吟醸

DESCRIPTION: A rich, fruity aroma complements the flavour of renowned Yamada Nishiki sake rice, bringing out smooth, well-balanced taste.

SERVING: Room temperature or chilled to 10°C.

RICE: Yamada Nishiki

POLISHING RATIO: 45%

ALCOHOL CONTENT: 16–17% by volume

PRODUCT NAME: Urakasumi Zen Junmai-ginjo
浦霞　禅　純米吟醸

DESCRIPTION: Mildly fragrant with a clean finish, this brew pairs wonderfully with food.

SERVING: Excellent served moderately chilled; when sipped at room temperature, a pleasant taste expands on the palate.

RICE: Toyo Nishiki and Yamada Nishiki

POLISHING RATIO: 50%

ALCOHOL CONTENT: 15–16% by volume

PRODUCT NAME: Urakasumi Junmai
浦霞　純米酒

DESCRIPTION: Marked by a clean taste with a rich flavour of rice.

SERVING: This wonderfully versatile sake can be enjoyed at room temperature, or chilled to 15°C. Slightly warmed, or fully warmed.

RICE: Manamusume

POLISHING RATIO: 65%

ALCOHOL CONTENT: 15–16% by volume

吉久保酒造　株式会社
Yoshikubo Sake Brewery
3-9-5 Honcho Mito-city
IBARAKI Japan 310-0815
www.ippin.co.jp
+81-29-224-4111
h.yoshikubo@ippin.co.jp

Yoshikubo 吉久保

Being carefully nurtured for over 230 years since the Edo period, this sake has been established as being refined for not only having a dry taste, but also for its sophisticated elegant flavour. Only a skilled craftsman who has gone through many years of training can create this kind of sake, the use of simple machinery cannot achieve the same standards.

The yeast that is used in this company has been handed down for generations, so it is nearly impossible for others to imitate the taste and aroma that the rice creates, which makes our sake have its own unique aromatic flavour.

The water that is used in the process of creating this sake was loved by Mitsukuni Tokugawa; a prominent daimyo in the Mito region in the early Edo Period, which is from the Kasahara water source where every morning we make sure to draw this spring water.

Traditional ingredients used in Japanese cuisine, including, glutamate, a high percentage of amino acid, amongst other ingredients makes our sake express its Japanese taste.

UG Sato, a worldwide graphic designer who created the Japan Airlines logo, and the Yakult logo amongst others, has worked with the Ippin Company for many years and has created many designs that are easily visible and fascinating for everyone.

吉久保 YOSHIKUBO

江戸時代から230年の歴史の中ではぐくまれた、洗練確立された我が社の日本酒は、辛口ながら旨味を感じる酒となっている。機械では醸す事の出来ない熟練職人技の酒である。酵母は古来より受け継がれた自社保存酵母を用い、米の旨味と味わい、そして香りの豊かな、他社には真似を出来ない、独特の酒造りを可能にしている。
仕込み水には、徳川光圀の愛した'笠原水源'の湧水を毎朝汲み、たっぷりと使い醸している。
日本の中でももっとも高い酸度、アミノ酸度を誇る純米大吟醸、純米吟醸、純米酒は、日本料理の出汁成分である、昆布由来グルタミン酸、鰹節由来イノシン酸、椎茸由来グアニル酸等と口の中に含む事により、日本一おいしさを感じることの出来る酒と言える。
　ラベル、パッケージデザイン等は日本航空や、ヤクルトのロゴマークを手掛けたU.Gサトーが手掛け、誰が見ても一目でわかり発音しやすいラベル、商品名となっている。

The Policy of 'Sake Ippin'

- Traditional and original brewing technique that has been used for 220 years.
- Persistently hand made.
- Our original yeast that continues evolving.
- The name of the brand 'Sake Ippin' has been kept since predecessors.
- Ippin is in the forefront in the world as a COOL JAPAN product.
- Products that can confront with beer and white wine.

一品のこだわり
①２２０余年続く、伝統的で独自の酒造り
②手造りにこだわる
③昔から進化し続けるオリジナルの酵母
④先代が残した『一品ｉｐｐｉｎ』というブランド名

Tasty looking Sake Ippin

Ippin- is an easily pronounceable and memorable name. We researched the name with 35 foreigners, and most of them said Ippin is easier to pronounce compared to other brands.

The logo is also unforgettable – 'one stick and three squares' It can be seen as a graphical image. The Chinese chacters of Ippin '一品' mean 'the best', 'excellent', 'the top'

It's known in Chinese character using countries such as Korea and China.

As mentioned above, it is easy to pronounce in English spoken countries.

一品の意味　'IPPIN (ONE AND ONLY)'
見た目も美味しい酒一品o
一品は、発音しやすく、覚えやすいブランド名。他社銘柄は、複雑なブランド名と感じる。
ブランド名、ラベルのマーケティングでは、どの国の言葉でも発音しやすく、One stick and three squaresとグラフィック的なイメージを持ち、アイキャッチがある。
☆中国、韓国等漢字圏では、一品の意味は、最上、最高、優れているの意味がある。
一品は、世界の日本酒で一番分かり易いブランド名である。

Flavourful Sake Ippin
Ippin Junmai & Ippin Junmai Ginjo
Ippin Junmai Ginjo　Asidity 1.50　Amino Acidity 1.40
Ippin Junmai　Asidity 1.90　Amino Acidity 1.80

The average of other brands
Junmai Ginjo　Asidity 1.37　Amino Acidity 1.32
Junmai　Asidity 1.53　Amino Acidity 1.66

Ippin has high acidity and amino acidity compared to other brands of sake in Japan. Stock is a must-ingredient in Japanese cuisine and is high in amino acids, (Bonito flakes, Konbu seaweed or shiitake mushrooms are well known as base materials.) So when swallowing the stock and Sake Ippin together, the flavour is enhanced.

Sushi, flavor of fish and soy sauce Amino acid
Soup, cooked dishes the flavour of raw material + stock + soy sauce
The national average　acidity 1.37　amino acidity1.32
Ippin Junmai　acidity 1.90　amino acidity1.80

Therefore Sake Ippin is a perfect match for Japanese cuisine. Flavourful and Enjoyable Sake Ippin.

PRODUCT NAME:	Junmai Daiginjo IPPIN 純米大吟醸 一品
AMOUNT:	720ml Unreleased in domestic market
RICE:	Yamada nishiki
DESCRIPTION:	It has a luxuriant scent and elegant sweetness like Godiva, but the price is still reasonable. 価格を抑え華やかな香りとゴディバの様な上品な甘みを感じるお酒です。

PRODUCT NAME:	Junmai IPPIN 純米酒一品
RICE:	Tamasakae
DESCRITPION:	It is called 'Eastern Chablis' and matches excellent with Oysters. カルフォルニアでは東洋のシャブリと称される生牡蠣と最高のマッチングの純米酒です。

1790: Established YOSHIKUBO SAKE BREWERY

Preparation of Ippin -start brewing from the first lucky day of November according to the almanac calendar, then non-stop for the whole Winter until spring.

- World recognized Sake Ippin
- Good design award
- Ibaraki Prefecture Good design award
- London Sake Challenge 2012 Gold and silver Bronze
  (Tournament that determines the sake of the world's best sommelier wine from around the world gathered in London)

BASICS

Preparing Rice 108

Preparing Rice for Sushi 109

Bonito and Kombu Dashi Stock 109

Fish Filleting 110

   Garfish Filleting 110

   Snapper Filleting 111

Sashimi Slicing Techniques 112

   Hiki-zukuri 112

   Sogi-zukuri 112

Preparing Rice

550 g/19 oz short grain rice

850 ml/30 fl oz water

1   Using the measuring cup provided with rice cooker, place of the rice into a bowl that will hold twice the volume of rice when cooked.

2   Pour water into bowl until it just covers the rice. Holding the bowl with one hand, stir rice briskly for 10–15 seconds with the other hand.

3   Carefully tip the milky water out, covering rice with one hand.

4   At the second and third rinse, add ample water and stir again for about 30 seconds to remove excess starch. Tip out water. Repeat with this action one more time.

5   Transfer rice to a fine-mesh sieve and leave to drain for 30 minutes.

6   Place rice and measured water into the rice cooker pan. Wipe the underneath of the pan with a dry towel and set it into the rice cooker. Switch on.

7   When cooked, leave for 10 minutes to steam.

8   Before serving, turn rice over gently with a moistened rice paddle to allow excess moisture to escape as steam.

Preparing Rice for Sushi

Use the opposite cooked rice
120 ml/4 fl oz rice vinegar
120 g/4 oz caster sugar
A pinch of salt

1   Prepare the vinegar mixture in a separate bowl, by combining the rice vinegar, sugar and salt. Make sure all ingredients are well mixed.

2   Transfer the hot cooked rice into a hangiri (flat wooden vessel) or a large wooden salad bowl. Pour in the vinegar mixture and work it through the rice using a wet wooden rice paddle. Gently mix the rice using the paddle's edge, taking care not to crush the grains of rice.

3   Cool the rice with a hand fan while mixing gently with the paddle in a slicing motion until the rice is at room temperature.

4   Do not refrigerate, as this dries out the sushi rice and causes the starch to break down.

Bonito and Kombu Dashi Stock

1 litre water
15 g/½ oz or 8 cm square Kombu (kelp) sheet
20 g/¾ oz Katsuo-bushi (bonito flakes)

1   Wipe kelp with dry cloth.

2   Put kelp in a pot of water and leave for half an hour.

3   Over low heat, bring it to the boil. Just as it boils, remove the kelp.

4   Add katsuo-bushi and remove from the heat.

5   Leave for 3 minutes and strain off over a bowl.

6   You may discard the katsuo-bushi or use for making miso dip.

To make Bonito Dashi, add katsuo-bushi into the boiling water and remove from the heat. Leave for about 3 minutes and strain off over a bowl.

Fish Filleting

Before filleting: Always check that your knife is sharp. If it is not, sharpen the blade before starting.

Garfish Filleting

This filleting method is quite similar to the three-piece filleting method.

1 Using a sharp knife, place blade behind gill and fin and remove head. Using the knife make an incision along the belly of fish, remove internal organs, then rinse fish thoroughly under running water.

2 With one hand holding the fish firmly, start cutting into the fillet from the (missing) head to the tail, along the back bone of the fish, lifting the fillet away as you cut. Turn fish over and repeat process.

3 You will now have 2 fillets, leaving the skeleton and bones which can be discarded.

4 Using your finger, peel the skin from each fillet.

*For larger fish, use tweezers to remove any remaining bones.

Snapper Filleting

This filleting is used for medium size fish.
For using skin, see page 179 'Snapper Skin Cracker'.

Approx. 1 kg/2½ lb sashimi quality Snapper

Note: If you want the skin to remain you will need to scale the fish before filleting. If not, the skin can be removed after filleting.

1 Scaling can often be a messy process, so work on a tray, at the sink or in a plastic bag. Holding head of fish and using a scaler, move scaler carefully against scales, working from tail to head. Rinse fish occasionally to make scaling easier.

2 If the fish has not been cleaned, use a sharp knife to make an incision along the belly of the fish, remove internal organs and rinse briefly. Lay fish down on board, place a knife behind gills and remove head. (The head can be used for 'Grilled Snapper Head').

3 With one hand holding the fish firmly, start cutting into the fillet from the (missing) head to the tail, along the backbone of the fish, lifting the fillet away as you cut. Place first fillet aside. Turn the fish over and repeat the process.

4 Use tweezers to remove any remaining bones that might remain in the fillets or around the visceral area.

5 You will now have 2 fillets, leaving the skeleton which can either be discarded or used to make fish stock.

6 (If you prefer to use the fillets without skin) Firstly, place the fillet skin side down onto cutting board, and insert knife just below the skin at the tail end. While supporting the fillet with your left hand, gently slice parallel to the chopping board with a smooth cutting action.

For using a snapper head, see recipe page 179.

leftover snapper head

1 Place the head on a cutting board. Hold the fish head firmly, then insert a knife, into the back of the head area which was attached to the body. Then carefully push the knife towards the front of the fish until the head can be opened into the shape of a butterfly. Or if desired, you can continue cutting so the head can be halved.

Sashimi Slicing Techniques

Sashimi slicing techniques vary according to the type of fish being used. Listed below are the two main techniques Hiki-zukuri and Sogi-zukuri.

Hiki-zukuri

For fish with thinner flesh, like snapper, this slicing method used is called 'Sogi-zukuri'.

Firstly cut your fillet, head end to tail end, into widths approx. 5 cm wide. Then, place the sectioned fillet onto a chopping board and hold with your left hand (reverse if you are left-handed). With a sashimi knife, slice the fish into pieces approx. 2.5 cm wide. After each slice is made, slide the cut piece along the cutting board, about 10 cm away from the fillet. Giving a slice 2.5 by 5 cm in size. Arrange the pieces neatly in a layered row.

Sogi-zukuri: Sashimi and Sushi tops.

For fish with thicker flesh, like tuna or salmon, the 'Hiki-zukuri' slicing method is used. This is the easiest sashimi slicing technique.

This slice is thinner than Hiki-zukuri sashimi. The thickness of the slice actually creates a different sensation in the mouth. Again, cut your fillet from head end to tail end into 5 cm wide pieces. Then, hold onto the thicker end of the fillet with your left hand (reverse if you are left-handed). Insert the sashimi knife at a 45-degree angle into the fish and slide the knife toward the left to make a thin slice about 2 mm wide. Giving a slice 2 mm by 5 cm slice.

OTSUMAMI (NIBBLING)
With sake as a starter

Edamame, Green Soy Beans..117
Grilled Edamame with Yukari Flavour 117
Fresh Oyster 117
Karasumi, Sun-Dried Mullet Roe 119
Mentaiko, Preserved Cod Roe with Chilli..119
Soba-Chips 121
Cream Cheese Flavoured with Saikyo Miso 121
Cream Cheese Flavoured with Wasabi..121
Prawn Miso Dip 122
Wasabi, Apple and Cheese Dip on Rice Crackers 122
Marinated Tofu Saikyo Miso and Mirin Flavour.................................123
Marinated Eggs Saikyo Miso and Mirin Flavour.................................123
Hiyayakko, Silken Tofu with Chopped Spring Onion and Bonito Flakes .. 125
Shredded Kelp Tsukudani with Rakkyo and Shichimi 125

Edamame, Green Soy Beans

1 bowl of fresh edamame beans (frozen beans are available from Japanese or Asian grocery shops) it is still rare to have fresh ones outside of Japan.

A pinch of salt

1 Heat a saucepan of water and add a pinch of salt.

2 Cook Edamame according to the packet and drain.

3 Sprinkle with freshly grounded salt.

=\\=\\=\\=\\=\\=\\=\\=\\=\\=\\=\\=\\=\\=\\=\\=

Grilled Edamame with Yukari Flavour

1 bowl of fresh edamame beans (frozen beans are available from Japanese or Asian grocery), defrosted

A pinch of salt

A pinch of Yukari (dried salted red shiso)

2 Dutch carrots, trimmed and peeled

1 Arrange defrosted Edamame on a baking tray.

2 Grill Edamame until cooked or lightly scorched.

3 Serve on a plate and sprinkle Yukari with Dutch carrot.

=\\=\\=\\=\\=\\=\\=\\=\\=\\=\\=\\=\\=\\=\\=\\=

Fresh Oyster

4 pacific oysters

Lemon or lime slice

1 Fresh oysters goes well with sake; the complex flavour of oysters meld smoothly with the mild crispness of sake.

Karasumi, Sun-Dried Mullet Roe

You can purchase karasumi from Japanese grocery shops.

Note: It takes about 3 weeks to make Karasumi at home.

A pair of fresh mullet roe, approx. 200~300 g/7–10½ oz

100 g/3½ oz sea salt

1 tablespoon sake or mirin

1 Prepare 5% salt water in a bowl and gently rinse the mullet roe.

2 Pat mullet roe with kitchen paper until dry and transfer into an air-tight container.

3 Before placing the lid on the container sprinkle the mirin or sake over mullet and add salt. Gently rub the salt over the roe and then seal the container with the lid and preserve for four days at room temperature.

4 After four days remove roe from container and use kitchen paper to gently pat off excess salt.

5 Place the roe on a flat surface (board or plate) and cover with a wire mesh food cover or sieve and place in a sunny position, occasionally turning them over, until semi-dried.

6 To serve, simply slice.

=⫻=⫻=⫻=⫻=⫻=⫻=⫻=⫻=⫻=⫻=⫻=⫻=⫻=⫻=⫻=

Mentaiko, Preserved Cod Roe with Chilli

You can purchase Mentaiko from Japanese or Korean grocery shops.

200 g/7 oz Cod roe

1 tablespoon mirin

40 g/1½ oz sea salt

20 g/¾ oz chilli powder

1 Prepare 5% salt water in a bowl and gently rinse the cod roe without damaging the outer layer of film/membrane. With kitchen paper gently pat off the excess water.

2 Place cod in an airtight container (without lid) and sprinkle with mirin.

3 Combine sea salt with chilli powder and gently coat the cod.

4 Place lid on container and refrigerate for 3 weeks until the roe becomes reddish colour.

5 You can enjoy mentaiko raw or lightly grilled.

Soba-Chips

200 g/7 oz dried soba noodle

1 tablespoon matcha mixed with 1 tablespoon salt

Vegetable oil for deep frying

1 Break soba noodle into half.

2 Prepare oil in a heavy pan and heat it up to 170°C/325°F.

3 Deep fry soba noodle until slightly brown.

4 Drain oil well on kitchen paper or wire mesh.

5 Serve on a plate with matcha salt

=/=

Cream Cheese Flavoured with Saikyo Miso

80 g/3 oz Cream cheese

70 g saikyo miso or 2 tablespoons common miso

70 g saikyo miso mirin

1 teaspoon caster sugar

1 teaspoon sake

1 Mix miso, mirin, sugar and sake in a container.

2 Coat the miso mixture around the cream cheese, leave for more than 1 hour.

3 Serve with crackers or vegetable sticks.

=/=

Cream Cheese Flavoured with Wasabi

80 g/3 oz Cream cheese

1 teaspoon–1 tablespoon wasabi paste as your preference

1 teaspoon mirin

1 teaspoon caster sugar

1 teaspoon sake

1 Mix wasabi paste, mirin, sugar and sake in a container.

2 Coat the wasabi mixture around the cream cheese, leave for 30 minutes.

3 Serve with crackers or vegetable sticks.

Prawn Miso Dip

140 g/5 oz cooked prawn meat
50 g/2 oz miso
1 tablespoon mirin
1 tablespoon sugar
1 tablespoon blue cheese
Salt to taste

1 Using a stick blender to mince the prawn meat. Add miso, mirin, sugar and blue cheese and blend. Taste with salt.

Alternatives: crab, lobster.

=¼=¼=¼=¼=¼=¼=¼=¼=¼=¼=¼=¼=¼=¼=¼=¼=

Wasabi, Apple and Cheese Dip on Rice Crackers

12 rice crackers
1 teaspoon wasabi paste
1 teaspoon cream cheese
1 (approx. 120 g/4½ oz) small Granny apple or Fuji apple, peeled, and cut into quarters, then soak in salted water (1 cup water and a pinch of salt)

1 Mix the wasabi paste and cream cheese in a bowl.

2 Grate the apple and transfer into the wasabi-cream, then mix well.

3 Serve the wasabi paste in a bowl with rice crackers.

Marinated Tofu Saikyo Miso and Mirin Flavour

100 g/3½ oz momen (hard) tofu

70g saikyo miso saikyo miso or 2 tablespoons common miso

1 teaspoon mirin

1 teaspoon sugar

1 Combine miso, mirin and sugar in a container.

2 Coat tofu with the miso mixture and refrigerate for 1 hour.

=⫻=⫻=⫻=⫻=⫻=⫻=⫻=⫻=⫻=⫻=⫻=⫻=⫻=⫻=⫻=⫻=

Marinated Eggs Saikyo Miso and Mirin Flavour

2 Boiled eggs, remove the shells

70 g saikyo miso saikyo miso or 2 tablespoons common miso

1 teaspoon mirin

1 teaspoon sugar

1 Combine miso, mirin and sugar in a container and marinate egg in the miso mixture.

2 Leave for 1 hour and cut into half.

Hiyayakko, Silken Tofu with Chopped Spring Onion and Bonito Flakes

SERVES 2

1 small packet of silken tofu, cut into 4

1 tablespoon spring onion or sliced shiso (Japanese green basil)

A pinch of katsuobushi (bonito flakes)

1 teaspoon grated ginger

Soy sauce for serving

1 Place the tofu into an individual bowl.

2 Top with spring onion or shiso, bonito flakes and ginger.

3 Serve with soy sauce

=/=/=/=/=/=/=/=/=/=/=/=/=/=/=/=/=/=/=

Shredded Kelp Tsukudani with Rakkyo and Shichimi

80 g/3 oz kelp

120 ml/4 fl oz water

60 ml/2 fl oz soy sauce

1 tablespoon mirin

50 g/2 oz caster sugar

1 tablespoon potato starch, dissolve with 1 tablespoon water

80 g/3 oz Rakkyo, pickled scallion

20 g/¾ oz shichimi, Japanese seven spices

1 Soak the kelp in water until slightly soft and with scissors cut into julienne.

2 Place the kelp in a pan, and add water, soy sauce, mirin and sugar. Bring it to the boil and simmer over low heat until the liquid has almost evaporated.

3 Add the potato starch mixture in the kelp and cook it through. Remove from the heat and cool it down in the room temperature.

4 Sprinkle shichimi and serve with skewered rakkyo on the side.

VEGETABLES

Pickled Daikon in Wasabi Flavour 128
Varieties of Pickles 128
Salted Pickles 129
Pickled in Shio-Konbu (Salted Kelp Strips) 129
Akajiso-zu (Japanese Red Basil Vinegar) Vinaigrette Pickles 130
Pickled Turnip in Wasabi and Sake Lee 130
Marinated Vegetables with Saikyo Miso, Mirin and Sake 131
Scorched Spring Onion with Chilli Miso 131
Grilled Vegetables 133
Grilled Sweet Chestnuts 135
Grilled Rice Cake with Miso and Nori Sheets 135
Grilled Tofu with Yuzu Miso 137
Grilled Varieties of Mushrooms 137
Grilled Konnyaku with Japanese Seven Spices 139
Tempura, Varieties of Fruits and Vegetables 139
Tofu and Shishitou Aspic 141
Vegetable Salad with Meringue Foam 143
Braised Burdock and Carrot with Sesame Flavour 143
King Prawn and Mushrooms in Dobin Tea Pot 145
Tofu Salad with Vegetables 145
Scorched Buckwheat with Miso Paste 146
Oden 147
Takenoko (Bamboo Shoot) Rice in Earthenware Pot 149
Furofuki Daikon in Broth with Hatcho-Miso 149
Rolled Gobo-Burdock with Kelp in Sansho Flavour 150
Stewed Turnip with Lemon Flavour and Kuzu Infuse 151

Pickled Daikon in Wasabi Flavour

200g/7 oz daikon, peeled and sliced

2 teaspoons wasabi paste

2 tablespoons rice vinegar

2 tablespoons caster sugar

1 teaspoon mirin

soy sauce for serving

1 Prepare the vinegar mixture, add wasabi, rice vinegar, sugar and mirin in a container and mix well.

2 Place the daikon slices in the mixture and toss with hands. Put a lid on and rest in the refrigerator for 2 hours.

3 Serve daikon in a plate with soy sauce.

=⫻=⫻=⫻=⫻=⫻=⫻=⫻=⫻=⫻=⫻=⫻=⫻=⫻=⫻=⫻=⫻=

Varieties of Pickles

60 g/2½ oz daikon radish, peeled and sliced

20 g/¾ oz kombu, sliced

1 teaspoon shio-koji (salted rice malt)

60 g/2½ oz carrot, peeled and julienned

2 tablespoons soy sauce

60 g/2½ oz Lebanese cucumber, partially peeled and sliced

½ teaspoon salt

2 red radish, trimmed, rinsed and cut into quarters

½ teaspoon

20 g/¾ oz sake kasu (sake lee)

1 teaspoon mirin

A pinch of salt

4 okra, trimmed

1 To make daikon pickle, place daikon, kelp and shiokoji in a zipped plastic bag and massage for 1 minute. Leave for 20 minutes in the refrigerator. When serving, rinse under running water and squeeze out the excess water.

2 To make carrot pickle, place carrot and soy sauce in a zipped plastic bag and massage for 1 minute. Leave for 20 minutes in the refrigerator. When serving, serve carrot pickle on a plate.

3 To make cucumber pickle, place cucumber and salt in a zipped plastic bag and shake to combine. Leave for 10 minutes in the refrigerator. When serving, rinse under running water and squeeze out excess water.

4 To make red radish, same as cucumber pickle.

5 To make okra pickle, add the sake kasu, mirin and salt in a zipped plastic bag and massage to combine. Add the okra and shake to combine. Leave for 20 minutes in the refrigerator. Serve in a bowl.

Salted Pickles

1 Lebanese cucumber, trimmed and sliced

A pinch of salt

Soy sauce for serving

1 Place the cucumber in a bowl and sprinkle salt.

2 Massage with fingers and set aside for 5 minutes. With hands squeeze out excess liquid.

3 Arrange cucumber in a bowl and aside with the ginger.

4 Serve with soy sauce.

=//=//=//=//=//=//=//=//=//=//=//=//=//=//=//=//=//=

Pickled in Shio-Konbu (Salted Kelp Strips)

1 celery stick

1 teaspoon shio-konbu, available from Japanese grocery shops

OPTION: add dried chilli, if you like spicy pickles

1 Cut the celery into 5 cm and slice into julienne.

2 Place celery in a container or a zipped plastic bag. Add shio-konbu.

3 Put a lid on and shake for a couple of minutes. Set aside for 30 minutes.

Akajiso-zu (Japanese Red Basil Vinegar) Vinaigrette Pickles

1 Japanese nasu-eggplant or ¼ egg plant

½ teaspoon salt

50ml akajiso-zu, available from Japanese grocery shops

1 Cut the egg into bite sizes. Place eggplant in a zip-closed plastic bag and sprinkle salt. Massage over the bag with hands and set aside about 15 minutes.

2 Add akajiso-zu in the bag and refrigerate overnight before serving.

=½=½=½=½=½=½=½=½=½=½=½=½=½=½=½=

Pickled Turnip in Wasabi and Sake Lee

200 g/7 oz baby turnips, peeled and sliced

1 teaspoon salt

2 tablespoons wasabi paste

80 g/3 oz sake kasu (sake lee), available from Japanese grocery shops

1 teaspoon caster sugar

1 tablespoon mirin

Soy sauce for serving

1 Rub turnip with salt with hands in a container.

2 Place the wasabi, sake-kasu, sugar and mirin in a blender and blend well.

3 Transfer the wasabi mixture into the turnip and preserve for more than 2 hours in the refrigerator.

4 Serve in a shallow bowl with soy sauce.

Marinated Vegetables with Saikyo Miso, Mirin and Sake

1 capsicum, halved and de-seeded

2 tablespoons saikyo miso

1 teaspoon mirin

1 teaspoon caster sugar

1 teaspoon sake

1　Combine saikyo-miso, mirin, sugar and sake in a container.

2　Coat the capsicum with miso mixture and leave for an hour.

3　Thinly slice from top to bottom before serving.

=//=//=//=//=//=//=//=//=//=//=//=//=//=//=//=//=//=

Scorched Spring Onion with Chilli Miso

8 (approx. 5 cm long) spring onion stems, choose the thick white part, trim

1 tablespoon sake

4 dried red chilli, halved and deseeded

4 tablespoons Hatcho-miso

1 tablespoon mirin

2 tablespoons honey

1 tablespoon Kuzu, Japanese potato starch or potato starch, mix with 1 tablespoon water

1　Sprinkle with sake over the spring onion.

2　Grill spring onion until scorched.

3　Add the chili, miso, mirin and honey in a pan and cook over low heat until simmering.

4　Add kuzu mixture to pan and stir for 1 minute or until cooked. Remove from the heat and pour glaze over the grilled spring onion.

Grilled Vegetables

1 small zucchini, trimmed and sliced into 8 round pieces

2 Dutch carrots, peeled and trimmed

2 asparagus spears, trimmed

1 Nasu (Japanese eggplant) or mini eggplant, halved lengthways and partially peeled

1 green onion, halved lengthways

1 tablespoon mirin

A pinch of salt

100 g/3½ oz butter, soften at room temperature

1 tablespoon soy sauce

6 bamboo skewers

1 Skewer carrot, eggplant, asparagus and green onion with a bamboo stick.

2 Skewer zucchini pieces with a bamboo stick.

3 Place the skewered vegetables on the baking tray.

4 Drizzle mirin and sprinkle salt over the vegetables.

5 Grill the vegetable under the grill until medium cooked.

6 Remove tray from grill, with a table knife spread butter over the vegetables and drizzle with soy sauce, return to the grill and brown for another 1 minute.

7 Serve on a plate.

Grilled Sweet Chestnuts

200 g/7 oz chestnuts

1 tablespoon mirin

2 tablespoons raw sugar

1 Preheat the oven 250°C/482°F.

2 With a knife make a crisscross slit on the surface of the chestnuts.

3 Spread chestnuts on the baking tray

4 Sprinkle mirin over the chestnuts.

5 Transfer the chestnuts to the oven and grill for 10 minutes.

6 Lower the oven temperature to 150°C/300°F.

7 Take out the chestnuts from the oven and sprinkle with sugar, and then place back in the oven. Grill for another 10 minutes or until the chestnuts partially open.

=/=/=/=/=/=/=/=/=/=/=/=/=/=/=/=/=/=

Grilled Rice Cake with Miso and Nori Sheets

8 approx. 3x3cm mochi, Japanese rice cake

4 3x12 cm nori sheets

2 tablespoons soy sauce

2 tablespoons caster sugar

40 g/1½ oz hatcho-miso

1 tablespoon sugar

1 tablespoon mirin

1 Prepare soy sauce mixture, mix the soy sauce and sugar in a bowl.

2 Prepare miso mixture, the haccho-miso, sugar and mirin in a bowl.

3 Grill 4 mochi cakes in the griller until puffy. Dip in the soy sauce mixture and wrap with a nori sheet.

4 Grill other 4 mochi cakes in the griller until puffy. Serve in a plate and graze with haccho-miso mixture.

Grilled Tofu with Yuzu Miso

200 g/7 oz momen-dofu (hard tofu)

YUZU-MISO

1 teaspoon yuzu powder
40 g/1½ oz saikyo (white) miso
1 tablespoon mirin
1 tablespoon caster sugar

1. To prepare tofu, place a thick sheet of kitchen paper or muslin cloth and tofu on a rack on a plate. Put a weight on top and stand for 15–20 minutes to discard excess water.

2. Transfer the tofu onto the chopping board and cut into four squares.

3. Lay baking paper on the baking tray and place the tofu.

4. To make yuzu miso, place the miso, mirin and sugar in a small pan and cook until all the sugar has dissolved.

5. Graze with yuzu-miso over the tofu. Grill until lightly scorched.

=\\=\\=\\=\\=\\=\\=\\=\\=\\=\\=\\=\\=\\=\\=\\=\\=\\=

Grilled Varieties of Mushrooms

2 tablespoons mirin
20 g/¾ oz Enoki-mushrooms
4 Shiitake-mushrooms
30 g/1 oz Eringe mushrooms
20 g/¾ oz shimeji mushrooms
1 tablespoon butter
1 tablespoon soy sauce
2 lemon wedges

1. Sprinkle mirin on top of mushrooms in a tray.

2. Transfer the tray into the griller and lightly grill.

3. Add butter and sprinkle soy sauce over the mushrooms.

4. Serve on a plate with a lemon wedge.

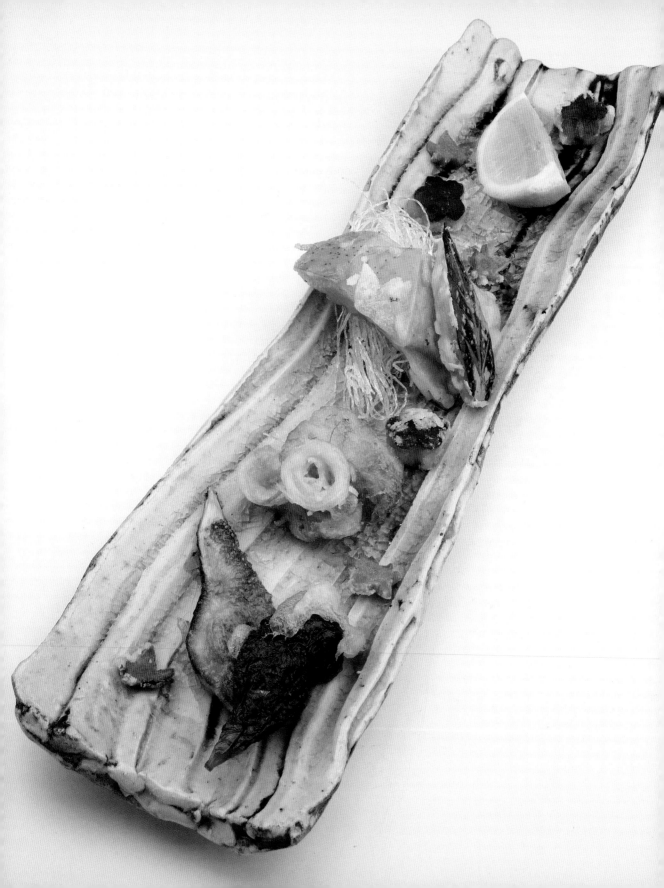

Grilled Konnyaku with Japanese Seven Spices

200 g/7 oz konnyaku

1 tablespoon mirin

1 teaspoon soy sauce

1 tablespoon shichimi, Japanese seven spices powder

1 teaspoon maple syrup

Vegetable oil

1   Cut the konnyaku into about 5 x 5 x 2 cm (thickness).

2   Drop oil in a pan and heat it up. Add the konnyaku and braise for 2 minutes over moderate heat.

3   Sprinkle mirin, soy sauce, shichimi and maple syrup and stir for another 2 minutes over low heat.

4   Serve on a plate.

=/=/=/=/=/=/=/=/=/=/=/=/=/=/=/=/=/=

Tempura, Varieties of Fruits and Vegetables

2 figs, halved

¼ mango, sliced into quarters

¼ Kaki persimmon, sliced into small pieces

¼ sliced onion rings

4 flower shaped peach and carrot

Potato starch for coating

40 g/1½ oz vermicelli

200 g/7 oz tempura flour

240 ml/8 fl oz cold water

Vegetable oil for deep-fry

OPTIONAL

2 teaspoon salt

1 teaspoon matcha

2 lemon wedges

1   Prepare the ingredients coated with potato starch and set aside.

2   To make tempura batter mix, place flour in a bowl. Add refrigerated cold water to make tempura crispy. Using a pair of chopsticks or fork gently combine.

3   Prepare oil in a tempura pan or a deep pan, such as a wok and heat to about 180°C/350°F.

4   To check the temperature, drop a small amount of the tempura batter into the oil, and when it quickly floats up, it is ready.

5   Holding one ingredient with a pair of long cooking chopsticks or tongs, carefully slide it into the oil.

6   Turn over when it becomes a light golden colour, and remove when cooked on both sides.

7   Drain on a wire rack or paper towel. Repeat with other ingredients.

8   Served with lemon wedges.

9   Combine with salt and matcha and serve with tempura.

Tofu and Shishitou Aspic

1 kanten stick (aga aga), approx.

500 ml/17½ fl oz bonito dashi

150 g/5 oz silken tofu, mashed

4 Shishitou, Japanese green chilli peppers, deseeded

8 Gouji seeds, soaked in water

1 teaspoon Usukuchi-shoyu (light colour soy sauce)

NOTE – a mould or dish will be needed, square or rectangular.

1 Rinse the kanten under running water and soak in a bowl of water for 30 minutes.

2 Place the dashi in a sauce pan and bring it to the boil.

3 Squeeze kanten and tear into pieces, then add the boiling dashi. Cook until dissolved well. Strain into another sauce pan.

4 Place the mashed tofu, shishifou, gouji and soy sauce in the dashi and bring it to the boil.

5 To prepare the square or rectangular mould, lay a sheet of cling wrap inside the mould. Spoon the mixture into the mould and refrigerate until set.

6 Remove the aspic from the refrigerator and, while carefully holding the corners of the cling wrap, transfer the set aspic to a chopping board. Remove cling wrap and slice into 4 pieces and serve on individual plates.

Vegetable Salad with Meringue Foam

SERVES 2

1 egg white

1 teaspoon soy sauce

1 teaspoon mirin

1 tablespoon sugar

A drop of rice bran oil

½ avocado, diced

½ mango, diced

40 g/1½ oz peeled carrot

40 g/1½ oz peeled daikon

½ spring onion, shredded and soaked in water

1 teaspoon roasted white sesame seeds

1 To make meringue, place the egg white in a clean bowl and whisk or beat with an electric hand mixer until soft peaks form.

2 To make dressing, add the soy sauce, mirin, sugar and oil in a small bottle or glass and mix well.

3 Place the avocado, carrot, daikon and spring onion in individual bowls and drizzle with the dressing, then spoon meringue on top. Lastly sprinkle sesame over the salad.

Braised Burdock and Carrot with Sesame Flavour

150 g/5 oz gobo (burdock), available fresh from Asian or Japanese grocery shops in season, otherwise use frozen as a substitute

50 g/2 oz carrot, peeled and julienned

1 tablespoon vegetable oil

1 tablespoon soy sauce

1 tablespoon mirin

1 teaspoon raw sugar

1 teaspoon sesame oil

1 teaspoon shichimi (Japanese seven spices)

1 To prepare the gobo, using the tip of the knife shave off the outer layer of burdock and cut into 5 cm and slice into julienne.

2 Drop vegetable oil in a frying pan and heat. Add burdock and carrot, and stir fry for 2 minutes over high heat.

3 Add soy sauce, mirin, sugar and sesame oil and stir, add the shichimi. Remove from the heat and serve in a small bowl.

King Prawn and Mushrooms in Dobin Tea Pot

2 fresh green whole king prawns, remove the shell and divide

2 mitsuba leaves (Japanese water cress)

2 dry shiitake mushrooms, soaked in water

40 g/1½ oz enoki mushrooms

40 shimeji mushrooms

480 ml/16 fl oz bonito dashi (see page 109)

2 teaspoons light colour soy sauce (usukuchi shoyu)

1 tablespoon mirin

A pinch of salt

2 Dobin tea pots or small ceramic tea pots

1 Place a king prawn into each teapot.

2 Arrange mitsuba, shiitake, enoki and shimeji mushrooms aside of the king prawn.

3 Combine dashi, soy sauce, mirin and salt together and pour into each teapot.

4 Top with a lid.

5 Set the pots on the stove and cook over low heat until full of flavour or for about 10 minutes.

6 Serve in the teapot.

Tofu Salad with Vegetables

100 g/3½ oz silken tofu

100 g/3½ oz carrot, peeled and julienned

4 stems baby broccoli, trimmed

50 g/2 oz miso

1 tablespoon mirin

1 Place kitchen paper and the tofu on a rack on a plate. Put a weight on top and stand for 15 minutes.

2 In the meantime, blanche the carrot and broccoli and refresh under running water. Combine miso and mirin in a bowl and toss the carrot and broccoli.

3 Pat tofu dry with kitchen paper and place into a bowl. Crush tofu with a spoon.

4 Add tofu into the carrot and broccoli, and toss together. Serve in a bowl.

Scorched Buckwheat with Miso Paste

100 g/3½ oz raw buckwheat
100 g/3½ oz Haccho-miso
40 g/1½ oz chopped chives
4 tablespoons lemon juice

1 Roast buckwheat in the oven (220°C/425°F) or in the pan until lightly roasted.

2 Cool it down.

3 Using the grinder, food processor or mortar and pestle, coarsely grind the buckwheat.

4 Place the buckwheat in a bowl and add the miso, sugar, chives and lemon juice, and then combine well.

5 Make the buckwheat mixture into a ball and place on the wooden ladle, then flatten. With a knife, make a crisscross pattern over the buckwheat.

6 Under the grill or using a blow torch, scorch over the buckwheat.

Oden

Oden is a popular stewed dish especially in winter time. The ingredients are quite versatile and in Japan there are shops that specialize in serving Oden dishes with sake, called 'Oden-ya' which are always crowded with people after work, dining or purchasing take-away meals for dinner at home.

The great varieties of fishpaste products used in these dishes are not as easy to find outside of Japan, but you can still enjoy Oden-ya style izakaya at home.

SERVES 4

8 cm long daikon, peeled, mentori-trimmed and cut into 2 cm slices

1 Konnyaku block, Konnyaku-potato gelatinous cake

4 small waxy type potatoes, such as Charlotte, peeled and soaked in water

4 hard-boiled eggs, peeled

2 Atsuage (Thick deep-fried tofu), cut in half diagonally

2 Abura-age (thin deep-fried tofu), pour on boiled water and cut in half lengthways

2 mochi (Japanese rice cake)

Fish paste products, such as chikuwa (cylinder-shape fish cake tube) or gobo-ten (deep-fried fish paste with burdock stick)

4 toothpicks

ODEN STOCK

1 litre dashi

4 tablespoons soy sauce

2 tablespoons mirin

2 tablespoons sake

A pinch of salt

Wagarashi or hot English mustard for serving

1. To prepare daikon, place daikon slices in a pan with water to cover. Bring to the boil and simmer for 15 minutes or until cooked.

2. To prepare konnyaku, cut in half and slice diagonally to make right-angle triangular shapes. Lightly score across one surface diagonally to allow flavour to be absorbed. Lightly boil.

3. To prepare potatoes, place in a pan with water to cover. Bring to the boil and cook for 10 minutes.

4. Prepare rolled cabbages and chicken balls.

5. Open abura-age from cut side, being careful not to tear, and insert mochi into each pocket. Using a toothpick as if sewing to close the pocket.

6. Prepare stock in a large pan. You may add chicken stock for extra flavour if you like.

7. Add daikon, konnyaku, boiled eggs, atsu-age, potatoes and fish products, and simmer for 20 minutes.

8. Add mochi and simmer another 15 minutes.

9. Serving in individual bowls with wagarashi.

Takenoko (Bamboo Shoot) Rice in Earthenware Pot

320 g/11 oz rice, rinsed and strained (see 'Preparing rice')

480 ml/16 fl oz bonito dashi (see page 109)

1 teaspoon light colour soy sauce

1 pinch of salt

100 g/3½ oz cooked bamboo shoots in a packet, sliced

2 dried shiitake mushrooms, soaked in water and sliced

A pinch of dry wakame seaweed

1 teaspoon sake

OPTIONAL
4 sprigs kinome (Japanese mountain pepper leaves), only available in season from Japanese grocery shops

1. See preparing rice. Place the rinsed rice in the earthenware pot.
2. Add the bonito dashi, soy sauce and salt.
3. Arrange the bamboo, the shiitake and wakame.
4. Sprinkle sake over.
5. Put a lid on and bring it to the boil over the medium heat until boiled.
6. Reduce to a low heat and cook for 10 minutes.
7. Remove from the heat and leave for 10 minutes to steam, and then serve.
8. Before serving, turn rice over gently with a moistened rice paddle to allow excess moisture to escape as steam.
9. Serve the rice in individual bowls, garnish with kinome sprig.

=/=

Furofuki Daikon in Broth with Hatcho-Miso

200 g/7 oz daikon radish

700 ml/24 fl oz bonito dashi (see page 109)

3 tablespoons sake

2 tablespoons Hatcho miso

2 tablespoons mirin

1 teaspoon caster sugar

1 teaspoon kuzu starch or potato starch, dissolved with 1 teaspoon water

2 stems shun-giku (edible chrysanthemum leaves)

1. To prepare daikon, peel and round off the edges and criss-cross score over the surface to allow the flavour to penetrate.
2. Place daikon in the pan and add dashi and sake, and then simmer until soft.
3. Meanwhile in a pan, add miso, mirin and caster sugar and combine well with a wooden spatula over low heat until sauce thickens and becomes slightly glossy. Remove from the heat.
4. Add chrysanthemum leaves with daikon, and add kuzu-mixture to make it thicken.
5. Serve daikon and chrysanthemum leaves in a shallow bowl with sauce.

Rolled Gobo-Burdock with Kelp in Sansho Flavour

80 g/3 oz fresh gobo-burdock available from Asian or Japanese grocery shops in season, otherwise use a frozen one as a substitute

950 ml/32 fl oz bonito stock

4 5x5cm kelp sheets, soaked in water

4 15 cm long Kanpyo (dried gourd strip), soaked in water

240 ml/8 fl oz soy sauce

2 tablespoons mirin

100 g/ 3½ oz caster sugar

1 teaspoon potato starch, dissolved with 1 teaspoon water

sansho powder, Japanese mountain pepper for seasoning

1 To prepare fresh Gobo-burdock, rinse and using the tip of knife shave off the outer layer of burdock. Cut to 6cm long and then julienne.

2   Place the dashi in a pan and place the gobo, bring it to the boil and simmer for 5 minutes.

3 Take out burdock and place onto a tray, allow to cool and then roll with kelp. Knot with the kanpyo string tightly.

4 Put the knotted burdock back to the pan, and add soy sauce, mirin and sugar. Bring it to the boil, and simmer until boiled down half of the the liquid, stirring occasionally without losing the form. Add the potato starch to thicken the sauce.

5 Serve in a small bowl and sprinkle with sansho powder.

Stewed Turnip with Lemon Flavour and Kuzu Infuse

4 small turnips approx. 60 g/2½ oz each, peeled

4 lemons

1 tablespoon mirin

1 tablespoon caster sugar

1 tablespoon kuzu-starch or potato starch, dissolved with 1 tablespoon water

Steamer

1. With a knife peel each turnip, keeping the stem.

2. To make a lemon basket, cut off the top ¼ of the lemon. And with a small spoon, scoop out the fruit into a bowl.

3. Insert a turnip into the lemon, repeat with other lemons and turnips.

4. Mix mirin, sugar and kuzu in a pan and cook until the sugar dissolves or it becomes clear.

5. Prepare the steamer and place lemon fruit in a lower pan with extra water. Set the upper steamer and place the lemon basket with turnip.

6. Spoon the kuzu sauce over the turnips.

7. Place a lid on and steam over a low heat until the turnips are cooked tender.

8. Serve on individual trays.

SUSHI AND SASHIMI

Simple Sashimi: Snapper Sashimi 155
Lobster Sashimi 157
Scampi Sashimi with Wasabi Tobikko and Finger Lime 159
Garfish Sashimi 159
Whiting Fillet Infused with Kelp Sheet 161
Fresh Oysters with Yuzu Gelee 163
Diced Glazed Tuna Sashimi withJapanese Taro Potato 163
Sushi: Nigiri-zushi 165
Slimy Mackerel Sushi in a Box 169

Simple Sashimi: Snapper Sashimi

2 snapper fillets, scaled with skin on (see basic 'snapper filleting')

120 g/4½ oz cucumber tsuma (see basic 'tsuma' page 157)

5 lemon slices, halved

Soy sauce for serving

Wasabi for serving

1 After scaling the snapper, remove any remaining bones with tweezers. Place snapper fillets on a platter or tray, skin side up. Pour boiling water over fish. When skin shrinks, transfer fish to a plate and refrigerate until cold. Before serving, slice fish in 'Hiki-zukuri style (see basics page 112).

2 Arrange cucumber tsuma on each serving plate. Slip lemon slices between pieces. Garnish with carrot with wasabi. Serve with soy sauce.

Lobster Sashimi

1 live lobster (700~1kg/1 lb 8 oz—2 lb)

80 g/3 oz sashimi quality salmon fillet, 1 cm x 1 cm x 8 cm long

40 g/1½ oz daikon, peeled like thin paper

1 lime or lemon, sliced

100 g/3½ oz Daikon tsuma*(see below)

Bowl of ice cubes

Soy sauce and wasabi for serving

1 Place the lobster into the freezer for approximately 10 minutes. This allows the lobster to go to sleep. Transfer to a cutting board.

2 Insert a sharp knife and cut through the lobster flesh where the tail meets the head. Carefully separate the head and tail of the lobster making sure no meat is left within the head.

3 Using scissors separate the top section of the tail from the bottom being careful to keep the bottom of the shell in once piece. Gently remove lobster flesh from the tail and chop into 2.5 cm pieces.

4 Place lobster pieces into the bowl of ice cubes. Allow to stand for 5 minutes to make the flesh crisp not frozen.

5 In the meantime, roll salmon with daikon strips. Slice into 4 pieces.

6 Remove lobster flesh from the ice and replace in shell. Arrange lobster on a plate.

7 Serve the lobster garnished with salmon rolled with daikon and lime slices.

8 Accompany with soy sauce and wasabi.

To prepare daikon-tsuma

1 x 10 cm long daikon, peeled

1 Using a vegetable-carving knife or paring knife, peel a section of daikon. Alternatively, use a peeler.

2 Place knife at a right angle to your work surface, cut daikon into very thin slices.

3 Separate slices and place in bowl of water, or refrigerate in water for 15 minutes. Drain well before using.

Or, using a vegetable peeler, cut daikon 20 cm long and slice off thin daikon strips. Then roll up and cut into thin julienne.

Scampi Sashimi with Wasabi Tobikko and Finger Lime

4 whole scampi, sashimi quality
2 tablespoons wasabi tobikko
2 finger limes, sliced
Soy sauce for serving

1 Separate the head and body of the scampi then, with cooking scissors, cut belly side open to remove meat. Transfer the flesh to the chopping board and cut into bite size pieces.

2 Arrange head and shells on a plate and place meat onto the shells.

3 Spoon wasabi tobikko over the flesh and top with finger lime slices.

4 Serve with soy sauce.

=/=/=/=/=/=/=/=/=/=/=/=/=/=/=/=/=/=/=/=

Garfish Sashimi

8 garfish fillets, for filleting (see Basics page 110)
4 teaspoons salmon roe caviar
Wasabi for serving
Soy sauce for serving
2 lemon wedges

1 Remove skin from fillets using fingers.

2 Cut each fillet along the centre line into 2 pieces.

3 Top each rolled garfish with caviar.

4 Serve with wasabi and soy sauce.

Whiting Fillet Infused with Kelp Sheet

4 small whole whiting

4 10x3cm kelp sheets, wiped with a dry cloth

2 tablespoons sake

1 teaspoon sea salt

2 flower shaped carrot baskets (see page 'red radish basket')

2 teaspoons wasabi paste

4 green shiso leaves (Japanese basil)

Soy sauce for serving

1   Fillet the whiting according to the basic technique, (Filleting Garfish see page 110), or ask the fishmonger when purchasing. There is no need to take off the skin, but you will need to remove the scales.

2   Place the fillets on a tray, skin side up. Sprinkle sake over the skin.

3   Layer up the 8 fillets with kelp sheet, one by one in a container and crack salt over.

4   Leave for 1 hour in the refrigerator.

5   Take out the piled fillets on the chopping board and cut into 3cm pieces together.

6   Serve on a plate and insert shiso leaves in-between whiting slices.

7   Serve with soy sauce.

Fresh Oysters with Yuzu Gelee

4g gelatine power, dissolved with 1 tablespoon water

1 tablespoon yuzu juice (Yuzu citrus)

1 teaspoon soy sauce

1 teaspoon mirin

60 ml/2 fl oz water

4 fresh pacific oysters

4 green shiso leaves (Japanese green basil)

1 Add gelatine, yuzu juice, soy sauce, mirin and water in a small pan and bring it to the boil.

2 Reduced the heat and cook until gelatine has dissolved. Transfer into a container and cool it down then refrigerate until set.

3 Rinse oysters in 5% salted water and drain well.

4 Transfer the yuzu gelle onto the chopping board. Cut into mini cubes.

5 Serve yuzu gelle as a side for the oyster with shiso.

Diced Glazed Tuna Sashimi with Japanese Taro potato

200 g/7 oz tuna, cut into 2.5cm cubes

100 g/3½ oz yama imo (Japanese Taro potato)

4 shiso leaves (Japanese green basil)

Wasabi for serving

Soy sauce for serving

1 Arrange the tuna cubes in a serving bowl.

2 Glaze the tuna with the yama-imo.

3 Place a shiso leaf on top of the tuna.

4 Serve with wasabi and soy sauce.

Sushi: Nigiri-zushi

To make 12 pieces of Nigiri-zushi

320 g/11 oz cooked sushi rice (see page 108)

2 king prawns, lightly cooked and allow to cool

2 sliced okra

4 slices salmon, cut using the sogi-zukuri (see page 112)

2 slices tuna, cut using the sogi-zukuri

2 slices kingfish, cut using the sogi-zukuri

2 snapper, cut using the sogi-zukuri

2 red radish (see page 166)

1 hard boiled egg yolk, sieved down to make egg mimosa

2 slices Japanese egg omelette (see page 167)

1 teaspoon wasabi

Soy sauce for serving

Gari, pickled ginger for serving

240 ml/8 fl oz water with 1 teaspoon rice vinegar

1 Wash your hands well, dip your fingers into the bowl of vinegared water, then clap your hands together to remove any excess water.

2 Pick up a slice of fish with your right hand and place it in your left, which is slightly cupped to hold the fish. (Reverse the hands if you are left-handed).

3 Pick up a slice with your right hand and place it in your left, which is slightly cupped to hold the fish. Using the tip of your right index finger, take a little wasabi and smear it on the fish.

4 With the fish in your left hand, grasp a little rice with your right hand (about 1 tablespoon). Rest the rice on the base of your fingers and squeeze lightly to form the rice into an oval-shaped pillow. Neaten the shape by turning the rice pillow around and pressing gently.

5 Transfer the rice onto the fish and press the fish and rice together. Hold your right index and middle fingers straight out together and place over the sushi then gently press. Turn over so the rice is now on top and gently press again. Turn over so the fish is on top again and press once more to complete.

To prepare king prawns

1 Remove the heads and rinse them under running water to clean. Remove the shell from the king prawns, keeping the tails with their bodies. From 0.5cm inside the neck part, insert a small knife from belly side toward back and gradually move the knife toward the tail. Open up like a butterfly and insert its head into the opened hole. Make nigiri and set on the plate, topped with king prawn. Arrange the sliced okra.

2 Arrange omelette, red raddish topped with egg mimosa.

3 Gari on the side of the plate and serve with soy sauce.

To prepare red radish

1 Make three thin cuts, spacing them evenly around radish. Make three more cuts about 1cm behind each first cut, making sure that the cuts meet near the bottom of the radish. Do not cut all the way through. Holding the bottom of the radish, gently cut off the top centre using the tip of knife. Place egg mimosa in the middle to create the pistil of the flower.

To prepare Japanese egg omelette

3 eggs

A pinch of salt

1 teaspoon caster sugar

1 tablespoon oil, soaked onto a piece of kitchen paper

Utensils, rectangular omelette pan (approx.: 13 x 19 cm) and maki-su (bamboo sushi mat)

1 Break eggs into a bowl and beat with a fork or chopsticks.

2 Add salt and sugar and stir well.

3 Spread the oiled kitchen paper over the surface and heat up over moderate heat.

4 Gently pour in a third of the mixture to cover base of omelette pan. Use a spatula to press out any air bubbles. When omelette sets and becomes dry, run a spatula around it to loosen.

5 With a spatula or chopsticks, fold one-third of the omelette from the far side towards the centre, then fold this over onto the remaining portion closest to you.

6 Using the oiled kitchen paper, wipe over the empty section of the pan, slide first omelette portion to the other end of the pan and pour in another third of mixture, lifting cooked omelette up to let it flow underneath.

7 When firm, fold the thicker portion over towards you as before, making a thick flat roll.

8 Continue adding mixture, cooking until firm and folding to make a triple-layer complete.

9 Remove from heat. Turn omelette onto a bamboo sushi mat.

10 Wrap the omelette with the sushi mat and shape it to a cylinder and fold with two rubber bands for 10 minutes.

11 Cut into pieces to serve. If possible use a heated iron seal to make a pattern.

Slimy Mackerel Sushi in a Box

300 g/10½ oz sashimi quality slimy mackerel (see 'Garfish filleting', page 110)

2 15x3cm kelp, wiped with dry cloth

1 tablespoon caster sugar

1 teaspoon sea salt

2 tablespoons rice vinegar

320 g/11 oz cooked prepared sushi rice

Soy sauce for serving

Wasabi for serving

A sushi mould, approx. 20 x 5 cm x 3 cm depth

Alternatively cake mould is used.

Bamboo leaves for garnish

1   For filleting, see 'Garfish filleting' page 110. Remove bones using tweezers.

2   Place fillets on a tray and sprinkle sea salt over the fillets, and then set aside in the refrigerator for 30 minutes.

3   Add sugar, rice vinegar and kelp in a container and transfer the fillets to the mixture. Leave for 30 minutes in the refrigerator.

4   Prepare a box shape sushi mould and place in the sushi rice. With a rice paddle flatten the top.

5   Take out the mackerel and pat with kitchen paper. Arrange mackerel fillet on top of sushi rice. Place a lid on and push the sushi over the lid to form.

6   Remove sushi out of the box and slice.

7   Serve on a plate with soy sauce and wasabi.

FISH

Pan Fried Sardines with Saikyo Miso, Mirin and Sake Flavour 172
Baby Octopus Tossed with Wakame and Sweet Miso 173
Pipi and Wakame Tossed with Sweet Miso 175
Grilled Fresh Oysters with Chilli and Sea Salt 175
Grilled Cod Fillet Marinated with Saikyo Miso 177
Grilled Snapper Head 179
Snapper Skin Cracker 179
Grilled Eel 181
Grilled Spanish Mackerel Cutlet
  with White Sesame Seeds and Lemon Wedges 182
Grilled Skewered Garfish 182
Grilled Slimy Mackerel in Miso Flavour 183
Grilled Giant Clam Stuffed with Sea Urchin 185
Grilled Sardine with Miso Flavour and Wrapped with Shiso Leaves 185
Grilled Sun Dried Garfish Fillet with Mirin Flavour 187
Grilled Sea Urchin in the Shell 187
Steamed Sea Urchin Custard in a Cup 188
Steamed Sea Urchin with Baby Turnips 189
Scorched Salmon with Asparagus Puree 191
Anago (Sea Eel) Tempura 191
Deep-Fried Whole Flounder 193
Deep-Fried Dressed Up King Prawn 195
King Prawn Crackers 197
Baby Octopus Crackers – Chilli Flavour 199
Deep-Fried Salmon Wrapped with Nori Served with Lemon Wedges 201
Snow Crab with Yuzu-Miso 203
Steamed Abalone in Sake with Grated Red Radish 205
Kinme-dai, Alfonsino in Broth 207
Kingfish and Daikon-Radish Cooked in Broth 208
Oysters with Hatcho-Miso in a Hot Pot 208
Cod Fishcake in Sweet and Sour Broth 209
Clam Rice 209
Salmon-chazuke 211
Sun Dried Whitebait Scorched with Aonori and Plum Vinegar 213
Snapper Red Miso Soup 213

Pan Fried Sardines with Saikyo Miso, Mirin and Sake Flavour

4 sardines

70 g saikyo miso

1 teaspoon mirin

1 teaspoon caster sugar

1 teaspoon sake

Potato starch for coating

1 tablespoon vegetable oil

1 Using a sharp knife make a slice along the belly of the fish and remove innards. Remove the head and rinse the remaining fish under running water. Insert a knife along the backbone and by moving the knife along the centre cut until the fish can be opened into the shape of a butterfly. Insert the knife from the tail along the centre bone and remove spine.

2 Place the fillets into the combined saikyo miso, mirin, sugar and sake and marinate for an hour.

3 Pat off the miso mixture and coat with potato starch.

4 Drop oil in a frying pan and heat it up, stir fry the sardine until cooked both sides.

Baby Octopus Tossed with wakame and sweet miso

200 g/7 oz baby octopus

40 g/1½ oz dried wakame seaweed, soaked in water

50 g/2 oz saikyo miso (white miso)

1 tablespoon mirin

1 tablespoon caster sugar

½ teaspoon Yuzu powder or lemon zest

1 tablespoon salt

1 To clean the octopus, remove guts from the octopus head.

2 Rub the octopus with salt.

3 Put some water in a pan and bring it to the boil.

4 Add the octopus and cook lightly.

5 Transfer the octopus to iced water and allow it to cool.

6 In the meantime, squeeze water from wakame and add to a bowl. Add miso, mirin and sugar and combine well.

7 Add the octopus in the bowl and toss.

8 Serve in a serving bowl and sprinkle with yuzu powder.

Pipi and Wakame Tossed with Sweet Miso

200 g/7 oz pipi

50 g/2 oz dry wakame, soaked in water and squeezed out

1 spring onion stem, blanched and chopped

70 g saikyo miso (white miso)

1 tablespoon mirin

1 teaspoon caster sugar

1 tablespoon salt

Yuzu powder for taste or lemon zest

1 Wash pipi with a bowl of salted water.

2 In a pan bring some water to the boil and blanch the pipi.

3 Take the pipi meat out of the shells.

4 Cut wakame into 2 cm.

5 Combine the miso, mirin and sugar in a bowl and add the pipi and wakame, and then toss together.

6 Serve in a bowl and sprinkle yuzu powder

=//=//=//=//=//=//=//=//=//=//=//=//=//=//=//=

Grilled Fresh Oysters with Chilli and Sea Salt

SERVES 4

12 fresh Pacific oysters in shells

1 teaspoon sake

60 g/2½ oz butter, cut into 12

2 tablespoons soy sauce

1 red fresh chilli, sliced

1 Gently rinse the fresh oyster in 5% salt water.

2 Lay the oysters on an oven tray and sprinkle with sake over them.

3 Prepare a griller and lightly grill.

4 Carefully transfer the oysters on a plate and top with butter and drop soy sauce over oysters.

5 Serve with sliced chilli.

Grilled Cod Fillet Marinated with Saikyo Miso

200 g/7 oz Cod fillet, cut into 2 pieces

A pinch of salt

80 g/3 oz saikyo miso (white miso)

1 tablespoon mirin

1 tablespoon caster sugar

4 wasabi leaves or water cress

Banana husk or bamboo husk for decoration

1 Sprinkle salt over the cod.

2 Mix saikyo-miso, mirin and caster sugar in a zipped plastic bag and marinate the cod. Refrigerate overnight.

3 Lightly pat off the miso from cod and grill until lightly brown on both sides.

4 Arrange banana husk on a plate. Place the cod and then top with wasabi leaves or water cress.

Grilled Snapper Head

SERVES 2

2 snapper heads, see 'Basics, Snapper filleting' page 111)

1 tablespoon sake

2 tablespoons sea salt

2 lime wedges

OPTIONAL:
2 tablespoons thinly sliced ginger julienne or fresh myoga (Japanese ginger) for condiment

1 To prepare the snapper heads, see Basics on page 111.

2 Arrange the snapper on a baking tray and sprinkle with sake and salt.

3 Grill the snapper until cooked and lightly scorched.

4 Serve with the lime wedges.

=/=/=/=/=/=/=/=/=/=/=/=/=/=/=/=/=/=/=

Snapper Skin Cracker

Approx. 100 g/3½ oz Snapper skin (see page 111 Snapper filleting)

2 tablespoons sake

2 tablespoons potato starch

1 tablespoon Aonori, green sea weed flakes

1 tablespoon sea salt

2 lemon wedges

Vegetable oil for deep-fry

Optional: soy sauce

1 With scissors or a knife, cut snapper skin into 5 x 5cm squares.

2 Sprinkle sake over the snapper skins on a tray.

3 Coat the snapper with the potato starch.

4 Prepare oil in a tempura pan or a deep heavy pan, such as a wok .

5 Heat up the oil to 170°C/325°F. Deep fry the snapper over the moderate heat until crispy.

6 Drain oil on a wire rack or kitchen paper.

7 Arrange on a plate and sprinkle salt and aonori.

8 Serve with lemon wedges and soy sauce.

Grilled Eel

About 60cm fresh eel

5 tablespoons mirin

2 tablespoons sake

6 tablespoons soy sauce

4 tablespoons sugar

Sansho pepper for serving

Kinome (Japanese mountain pepper) spring

8 bamboo sticks

1 To prepare, wipe the eel with kitchen paper to remove slime from the skin.

2 Place the eel on a chopping board, cut off the head. Cut eel into 10cm slices and insert the knife from the backside of the eel along the bone. Moving the knife to open up like a butterfly. Turn the eel over and insert the knife along the bone, gently moving the knife cut it off at the centre bone. Repeat with the other pieces. Rinse under running water and pat with kitchen paper. Skewer the fillet on both the left and right side of the skin to prevent curling when grilling. Refrigerate until used.

   * Professional eel chefs fillet live eels skilfully, it needs lots of experience to handle a slimy live eel.

3 To prepare sauce, lightly grill the eel head and bones. Add mirin and sake in a medium size pan and bring it to the boil. Add soy sauce and sugar and simmer for 5 minutes over low heat. Place eel head and bones in the sauce and simmer for 10 minutes. Sieve the sauce and set aside.

4 Grill the eels or barbecue over a medium heat, brushing both sides with the sauce occasionally at least 5 times during cooking.

5 Serve on a plate and sprinkle the sansho pepper or kinome spring.

NOTE: Grilled eel is good for both Sushi and Unajyu (grilled eel with steamed rice in a container)

魚 FISH

Grilled Spanish Mackerel Cutlet with White Sesame Seeds and Lemon Wedges

200 g/7 oz Spanish mackerel cutlet
1 tablespoon sake
1 teaspoon sea salt
1 tablespoon roasted white sesame seeds
4 lemon wedges

1 Sprinkle sake over the mackerel and sprinkle salt.

2 Place mackerel on a baking tray and grill until cooked medium.

3 Take the mackerel out and sprinkle sesame seeds. Put it back in the griller and grill until lightly golden.

4 Serve with lemon wedges

=⫻=⫻=⫻=⫻=⫻=⫻=⫻=⫻=⫻=⫻=⫻=⫻=⫻=⫻=⫻=

Grilled Skewered Garfish

4 whole garfish, about 100 g/3½ oz each
2 tablespoons mirin
½ tablespoon salt
Soy sauce for serving
2 lemon wedges
4 x 25 cm Metal skewers

1 Remove scales from garfish using a scaler or knife. Make a slit on the belly side and remove guts and gills. Rinse under running water.

2 Insert a metal skewer through the mouth of each fish along the length of the belly, coming out at the tail, using a weaving motion. Sprinkle with mirin and salt.

3 Heat barbecue grill or griller.

4 When the skin becomes crispy, using a glove or a towel remove from the slats and serve on a plate.

5 Serve with lemon wedges and soy sauce.

Grilled Slimy Mackerel in Miso Flavour

300 g/10½ oz fresh slimy mackerel, to fillet (see basic 'Garfish filleting' page 110)

50 g/2 oz miso

2 tablespoons mirin

1 tablespoon caster sugar

1 tablespoon shiso leaves

20 g/2 oz ginger, peeled and grated

1 Fillet the mackerel according to the 'Garfish filleting' into 2 pieces.

2 To make the marinade mixture, mix miso, mirin and sugar in a tray and place the mackerel.

3 Coat the mackerel with miso mixture and leave for 3 hours in a refrigerator.

4 Transfer the mackerel into the griller and grill until medium grilled.

5 Serve with grated ginger.

魚 FISH

Grilled Giant Clam Stuffed with Sea Urchin

4 giant clams	1 With butter knife, open up the clams.
140 g/5 oz sea urchin raw	2 Remove flesh from the clams.
2 tablespoons mirin	3 Remove guts and rinse in 5% salted water.
A pinch of salt	4 Place flesh back into shell and arrange sea urchin on top.
4 kinome sprigs, Japanese mountain pepper sprigs	5 Sprinkle mirin over and grill over low heat until slightly scorched on the sea urchin.
	6 Arrange kinome sprigs on the sea urchin and place another shell on top.

=\|=\|=\|=\|=\|=\|=\|=\|=\|=\|=\|=\|=\|=\|=\|=\|=

Grilled Sardine with Miso Flavour and Wrapped with Shiso Leaves

200 g/7 oz sardine	1 Butterfly sardines.
50 g/2 oz miso paste	2 Combine miso and mirin in a container and transfer the sardines. Marinade for 30 minutes.
2 tablespoons mirin	
4 shiso, Japanese basil leaves	3 Transfer the sardine onto a baking tray and grill at moderate heat for 5 minutes or until halfway cooked.
	4 Take out the sardines and wrap each sardine in a shiso leaf.
	5 Place back the sardine in the griller and grill until cooked.

Grilled Sun Dried Garfish Fillet with Mirin Flavour

4 large garfishes,

4 tablespoons mirin

2 teaspoons sea salt

Soy sauce for serving

1 To fillet the garfish, with a sharp knife, remove the head off the fish and trim off the belly side to gut out. Rinse under the running water. Insert the tip of the knife and start cutting into the fillet from the (missing) head to the tail, along the backbone of the fish, from the shoulder part and slide the knife along the centre bone. Turn over the fish and repeat with other side. Open up the butterfly, cut off the bone and discard.

2 Sprinkle salt over the garfish and leave for 10 minutes.

3 Brush the garfish with mirin.

4 Place fish on a mesh and brush with mirin over the fish several times.

5 Use a mesh hanging box with dipper or a mesh washing bag. Transfer the fish to the box or bag and then hang in a good breeze for a day.

6 Take out the fish and grill until cooked.

=//=//=//=//=//=//=//=//=//=//=//=//=//=//=//=

Grilled Sea Urchin in the Shell

4 whole sea urchins

2 tablespoons sake

2 tablespoons soy sauce

2 kinome sprigs (Japanese mountain pepper sprigs)

1 Prepare whole sea urchin by cutting a little off the top.

2 Remove raw out of the shell.

3 Rinse the shells under running water and place back raw into the shells.

4 Arrange the sea urchin on a baking tray.

5 Sprinkle Sake and soy sauce over the roe.

6 Grill the sea urchin until lightly cooked.

7 Serve the sea urchin topped with kinome sprig on a plate with a spoon.

Steamed Sea Urchin Custard in a Cup

SERVES 2

2 eggs, beaten

240 ml/8 fl oz bonito dashi (see page 109)

1 teaspoon light colour soy sauce

1 teaspoon mirin

100 g/3½ oz sea urchin roe

2 kuko, goji seeds

2 mitsuba (Japanese water cress) leaves

1 Bring water in a steamer to the boil, then reduce heat to simmer.

2 Meanwhile, prepare egg mixture by combining egg, dashi, soy sauce and mirin in a bowl.

3 Strain egg mixture and pour into 2 cups.

4 Place the sea urchin and kuko into each cup.

5 Cover each cup with a piece of foil. Carefully place them into the steamer. Steam over low heat for approx. 10 minutes. To check if cooked, insert a skewer into the egg. If ready, clear juice will appear on the surface. Just before serving top with a mitsuba leaf.

Steamed Sea Urchin with Baby Turnips

4 turnip, approx. 60 g/2½ oz each

40 g/1½ oz sea urchin roe

950 ml/32 fl oz bonito stock (see page 109)

2 tablespoons mirin

A pinch of sea salt

1 tablespoon soy sauce

1 With a small knife, peel the turnips from the stem to the bottom, keeping the shape round as you go, leaving stem attached.

2 Prepare a steamer and add the bonito stock to the pan. Arrange the turnip on a steamer with a lid on. Bring it to boil and steam over low heat until half way cooked or for 10 minutes.

3 Turn the heat off and remove the lid. Place the sea urchin on top of the turnip and sprinkle with mirin and sea salt. Place back the lid and steam for 5 minutes over the low heat.

4 Serve on a plate with soy sauce.

魚 FISH

Scorched Salmon with Asparagus Puree

4 asparagus spears, trimmed and blanched

1 tablespoon mirin

A pinch of salt

1 tablespoon sour cream

200 g/7 oz salmon fillet, diced (2cmx2cm cubic)

10 capers

Blow torch for browning

1 Cut asparagus in half and use bottom parts for puree.

2 To make asparagus puree, add the asparagus bottom parts (except for very end), mirin, salt and sour cream in a food processor and blend until creamy texture.

3 Place salmon cubes on a tray and, with a blow torch, scorch over the surfaces.

4 Arrange scorched salmon pieces on a plate.

5 Spoon asparagus puree over the salmon and insert asparagus tops.

6 Garnish with capers around the salmon.

=/=/=/=/=/=/=/=/=/=/=/=/=/=/=/=/=/=

Anago (Sea Eel) Tempura

SERVES 4

4 Anago (sea eel) fillets, approx. 90 g/3½ oz each or you can purchase frozen sea eel

Potato starch for coating

160 g/5½ oz Tempura flour

160 ml/5½ fl oz cold water

½ tablespoon matcha, combine with ½ tablespoon salt

4 lime or lemon wedges

Vegetable oil for deep fry, approx. ½ oil in a pan

1 For filleting the sea eel, it is better to ask a fishmonger when you purchase or see 'Basics' on page 110–111.

2 Coat the eel fillets with the potato starch and set for 10 minutes.

3 In the meantime, add the tempura flour and water in a bowl and lightly stir.

4 Prepare the oil in a tempura pan or a heavy deep pan, such as a wok and heat up to 180°C/350°F.

5 Dip the coated eel fillet in the tempura flour one by one and gently slide into the heated oil. Deep-fry until it is golden brown, turning occasionally with a pair of saibashi (cooking long chopsticks) or tong. Remove tempura from the oil and drain on wire rack or kitchen paper.

6 Serve while it is warm with matcha salt and lime wedges.

Deep-Fried Whole Flounder

2 whole small flounders (approx. 300 g/10½ oz each)

4 tablespoons sake

120 ml/4 fl oz water

2 flower shaped daikon pieces

2 flower shaped carrot pieces

60 g/2½ oz shimeji mushroom, trimmed

1 teaspoon soy sauce

1 tablespoon rice vinegar

1 tablespoon caster sugar

40 g/1½ oz sliced ginger

1 tablespoon potato starch, dissolved with 2 tablespoons water

Potato starch to coat

1 tablespoon dry wakame seaweed

2 green shiso (Japanese basil), deep fried

Vegetable oil for deep fry

1. Prepare the flounder; remove the scales with a scaler or with a knife and rinse.

2. Pat the flounder with kitchen paper to remove any excess water.

3. With a knife, make crisscross slits on the surface. Sprinkle sake over the flounder and leave in refrigerator until cooking time.

4. To prepare Ankake-sauce, place water, carrot and daikon in a saucepan and bring to the boil, then cook for 2 minutes over low heat. Add shimeji mushroom, soy sauce, rice vinegar, caster sugar and simmer for a couple minutes. Finally place sliced ginger. Add potato starch to thicken. Remove pan from heat and set aside.

5. Before deep-frying flounder, place potato starch in a tray or plate and lightly coat fish.

6. Prepare oil in a tempura pot or heavy deep pot (such as a wok) and heat to around 180°C/350°F. Carefully slide each flounder into the oil one at the time and turn over when it becomes a light golden colour, deep-fry both sides until crispy. Allow oil to drain by placing cooked fish on a wire rack or kitchen paper. Repeat with another flounder.

7. Arrange each flounder on a plate and spoon Ankake-sauce over.

8. Top with deep-fried green shiso.

Deep-Fried Dressed Up King Prawn

4 large green prawns

2 tablespoon potato starch

1 egg, beaten

80 g/3 oz Shinbiki-ko (roasted puff rice), available from Japanese grocery shops

1 teaspoon matcha (green tea powder)

1 teaspoon sea salt

Vegetable oil for deep frying

1 To prepare the prawns, first shell and devein. Then make a shallow incision, from left to right into the underside of prawns, which allow the prawns to lay flat.

2 Place potato starch, egg and shinbiki-ko into separate bowls.

3 Coat prawns first with potato starch. Then dip into egg and lastly cover with shinbiki-ko and press to stick.

4 Prepare oil in a tempura pot or heavy deep pot (such as a wok) and heat to around 180°C/350°F. Carefully slide each prawn into the oil and turn over when they become a light golden colour, deep-fry until crispy. Drain off excess oil by placing cooked prawns on a wire rack or kitchen paper.

5 Combine matcha and salt together and serve by sprinkling over the king prawns.

King Prawn Crackers

8 green king prawns

2 tablespoons soy sauce

1 tablespoon mirin

1 tablespoon caster sugar

Potato starch for coating (approx. 3–4 tablespoons)

4 tablespoons chopped green shiso (Japanese green basil)

4 lemon wedges

Vegetable oil for deep frying

1   To prepare the king prawns; with a knife make a cut along the belly side (leave shell on) and open up like a butterfly. Place a cotton cloth over the prawn and with the back of the knife, or a pounder, gently beat till flat.

2   Add soy sauce, mirin and caster sugar in a container and marinate the prawns for 30 minutes.

3   Pat the king prawns with kitchen paper until dry. Coat with potato starch and spread chopped shiso over the flesh side.

4   Prepare oil in a tempura pan or deep pan (such as a wok) and heat to about 170°C/325°F.

5   Carefully slide each prawn into the oil and turn over when it becomes light golden colour, deep-fry both sides until crispy. Drain off excess oil by placing cooked prawns on a wire rack or kitchen paper.

6   Serve with lemon wedges.

魚 FISH

Baby Octopus Crackers – Chilli Flavour

200 g/7 oz baby octopus

2 tablespoons shichimi pepper, Japanese seven spices

2 tablespoons soy sauce

2 tablespoons mirin

2 tablespoons caster sugar

4 tablespoons of steamed sticky rice

Potato starch for coating (approx. 2 tablespoons)

Roasted white sesame seeds are optional.

1 To prepare the octopus, use a sharp knife to make a cut through the hood and open up like a butterfly. Remove any intestinal track from the head and rinse under the running water. Wipe thoroughly dry with kitchen paper.

2 With a knife make several shallow crisscross cuts through the flesh of the hood.

3 Place a cotton cloth over the octopus. Using the back of knife or a pounder, gently beat until flat.

4 Combine soy sauce, mirin and caster sugar in a container and marinade the octopus for 30 minutes.

5 Wipe octopus dry with kitchen paper.

6 Place sticky rice into butterflied section of octopus.

7 Lightly coat octopus with potato starch.

8 Prepare oil in a tempura pan or deep pan (such as a wok) and heat to about 170°C/325°F.

9 Carefully slide octopus into the oil and turn over when they become a light golden colour, deep-fry both until crispy. Drain excess oil from cooked octopus by placing on a wire rack or kitchen paper.

10 To serve sprinkle with shichimi.

Deep-Fried Salmon Wrapped with Nori Served with Lemon Wedges

200 g/7 oz salmon fillet without skin, cut into bite size pieces

10 5cm x 5cm nori sheets

Potato starch for coating (approx. 2 tablespoons)

Sea salt for taste

2 lemon wedges

Vegetable oil for deep-fry

1　Wrap the salmon with a moistened nori sheet leaving only one part of the fish exposed.

2　Coat with potato starch.

3　Prepare oil in a tempura pan or deep pan (such as a wok) and heat to about 170°C/325°F.

4　Carefully slide it into the oil and turn over when it becomes light golden colour, deep-fry until crispy. Drain off excess oil by placing on a wire rack or kitchen paper.

5　Sprinkle with sea salt while hot.

6　Serve with lemon wedges.

魚 FISH

Snow Crab with Yuzu-Miso

SERVES 2

1 teaspoon yuzu juice, yuzu citrus juice available from Japanese grocery shop

40 g/1½ oz miso

1 tablespoon mirin

1 tablespoon caster sugar

2 green shiso leaves

400 g/14 oz cooked snow crab legs

1   To make Yuzu-miso, add yuzu juice, mirin and caster sugar in a small pan and heat it up until well combined.

2   With cooking scissors, cut off each joins and open up one side of the shell.

3   Serve on a plate with yuzu-miso and shiso leaves.

Steamed Abalone in Sake with Grated Red Radish

2 Abalone

A pinch of salt

240 ml/8 fl oz sake

2 10x10cm kombu (kombu kelp) sheets

2 carrot peeled strips

2 flower shaped flowers

1 tablespoon mirin

2 red radish, trimmed and grated

1 Sprinkle salt over the abalone and leave for 10 minutes, and rinse under running water.

2 With a butter knife, remove the flesh and livers.

3 Put flesh on the chopping board and with a small knife make crisscross patterns over to absorb the flavour of the sake.

4 Prepare a steamer and add sake in the pot and set mesh over it.

5 Arrange kelp sheet onto the shells and place abalones flesh and livers. Top with daikon and carrot. Sprinkle mirin over the abalones.

6 Steam for 10 minutes. Serve with grated red daikon.

Kinme-dai, Alfonsino in Broth

2 whole kinme-dai, approx. 200 g/7 oz each

2 tablespoons mirin

2 tablespoons sake

4 tablespoons soy sauce

1 tablespoon caster sugar

A pinch of salt

480 ml/16 fl oz bonito dashi (see page 109)

20 g/¾ oz fresh ginger, julienned

2 knots of spring onion

1 To prepare Kinme-dai, with a scaler remove the scales in a plastic bag. Rinse under running water, place on a chopping board and with a knife slit cross belly of fish, remove viscera and rinse briefly. Pat the fish with kitchen paper.

2 Add mirin, sake, soy sauce, sugar, ginger, salt and dashi in a pan and place Kinme-dai. Top with a lid or a piece of baking paper.

3 Bring it to the boil and simmer over low heat for about 30 minutes or cooked.

4 Serve the kinme-dai with the sauce and spring onion in a soup plate.

魚 FISH

Kingfish and Daikon-Radish Cooked in Broth

200 g/7 oz kingfish cutlets

2 tablespoons sake

100 g/3½ oz daikon

950 ml/32 fl oz dashi (see basics page 109)

1 tablespoon mirn

1 tablespoon usukuchi-shoyu, light colour soy sauce

A pinch of salt

1 tablespoon wagarashi or English mustard

1 Sprinkle sake over the kingfish.

2 Peel the daikon and slice into 1 cm pieces. Round off the edges and make criss-cross scoring over the surface to allow the flavour to penetrate.

3 Place the kingfish and daikon in a pan.

4 Add dashi, mirin and soy sauce and simmer over moderate heat until the daikon cooked.

5 Add the salt and cook a couple of minutes over the low heat.

6 Serve with the wagarashi.

=//=//=//=//=//=//=//=//=//=//=//=//=//=//=//=//=//=//=

Oyster with Hatcho-Miso in a Hot Pot

80 g/3 oz momen (hard) tofu, cut into approx. 3 x 3 cm cubes

100 g/3 ½ oz Hatcho-miso

3 tablespoons caster sugar

1 tablespoon mirin

1 dozen fresh pacific oysters, rinse in a bowl of salt water (5% salt)

950 ml/32 fl oz dashi (see page 109)

2 stems edible chrysanthemum leaves, trimmed and chopped

1 stem spring onion, trimmed and chopped

Do-nabe (Earthenware pot), iron pot or other pot

Use a portable stove

1 Arrange tofu on a baking tray and lightly grill or using a blowtorch scorch over the surface.

2 Place miso, sugar and mirin in a bowl and combine well. Smear miso mixture around the top edge of do-nabe.

3 Pour dashi and bring it to the boil. Place tofu and oyster.

4 Place the chrysanthemum leaves and spring onion.

5 Cook over the moderate heat before boiling.

6 Transfer the pot onto the portable stove at the table.

Cod Fishcake in Sweet and Sour Broth

200 g/7 oz minced cod

80 g/3 oz momen (hard) tofu

1 carrot, peeled and finely chopped

2 dried shiitake mushrooms, soaked in water and thinly sliced

1 tablespoon mirin

1 tablespoon usukuchi-shoyu, light colour soy sauce

A pinch of salt

3 tablespoons katakuri-ko (potato starch) for coating

Vegetable oil for deep frying

480 ml/16 fl oz dashi (see page 109)

1 tablespoon mirin

1 tablespoon caster sugar

1 teaspoon rice vinegar

1 Place the cod, tofu, carrot, shiitake, mirin, soy sauce and salt in a bowl. Combine well by hand. Divide into 8 pieces and shape them into round oval shapes.

2 Coat with potato starch and set for a couple of minutes.

3 Prepare oil in a tempura pan or deep pan (such as a wok) and heat to about 170°C/325°F.

4 Carefully slide it into the oil and turn over when it becomes light golden colour, and deep-fry both sides. Drain oil on a wire rack or kitchen paper. Repeat with other ingredients.

5 Place the dashi, mirin, sugar and vinegar in a saucepan and bring it to the boil. Transfer the deep-fried cod. Simmer for 20 minutes.

6 Serve deep-fried cod in a bowl with broth.

=//=//=//=//=//=//=//=//=//=//=//=//=//=//=//=//=//=

Clam Rice

320 g/11 oz short grain rice

160 g/5½ oz clam meat

1 tablespoon sake

480 ml/16 fl oz bonito dashi (see page 109)

1 teaspoon usukuchi-shoyu, light colour soy sauce

1 teaspoon yukari, salted dry red shiso flakes

4 mitsuba leaves, Japanese water cress

1 To prepare rice, see basics page 108 and prepare rice in the rice cooker.

2 Add clam meat, sake and dashi, and soy sauce. Leave for 30 minutes.

3 Cook rice. When it is cooked, steam for 15 minutes.

4 Before serving, sprinkle yukari and place mitsuba and steam for another 5 minutes.

5 Serve in individual rice bowls.

Salmon-chazuke

200 g/7 oz salmon fillet

1 teaspoon freshly grounded salt

2 bowls of cooked rice separately in an individual bowl

2 umeboshi (salted pickled plum)

1 nori sheet, cut into strips

1 teaspoon roasted white sesame seeds

1 teaspoon chopped spring onion

Prepare ban-cha or hoji-cha green tea in a teapot

1 Place the salmon and sprinkle salt over the salmon. Grill until well cooked.

2 Cool it down. With hands, separate the salmon into flakes.

3 On a bowl of rice, place flaked salmon and top with the umeboshi, nori, sesame seeds and spring onion.

4 Pour the tea over the nori before eating.

魚 FISH

Sun Dried Whitebait Scorched with Aonori and Plum Vinegar

4 sheets white bait, sun dried or frozen available from Japanese grocery shops

2 tablespoons mirin

2 tablespoons aonori, green nori flakes

2 tablespoons bainiku, salted plum paste

1 tablespoon rice vinegar

1 tablespoon caster sugar

1 Sprinkle mirin over the sun-dried white bait sheets on a baking tray.

2 Sprinkle aonori.

3 Lightly scorch in a griller both sides until crispy.

4 Mix the bainiku, rice vinegar and sugar in a bowl.

5 Spread the mixture over the white baits sheets.

6 Transfer white baits sheets on a chopping board and slice into bite sizes.

=/=/=/=/=/=/=/=/=/=/=/=/=/=/=/=/=/=

Snapper Red Miso Soup

2 snapper collars (see basic page 111)

2 tablespoons sake

700 ml/24 fl oz water

2 tablespoons Hatcho-miso, dissolved with 1 tablespoon mirin

2 tablespoons chopped chives

Salt to taste

1 Place the snapper collars in a baking tray and sprinkle with sake, then lightly grill.

2 Add water to a pot and transfer snapper.

3 Cook over a low heat for 3 minutes.

4 Add the hatcho-miso mixture into the soup and cook another 1 minute.

5 Transfer snapper collars into individual soup bowls.

6 Add soup over snapper.

7 Sprinkle chives before serving.

MEAT AND POULTRY

Diced Pork in Broth...217
Deep-Fried Crispy Pork with Shichimi Salt............................217
Stir-Fried Rolled Pork with Shishitou.....................................218
Pork Shabu-Shabu Salad...218
Kushi-age, Deep-Fried Skewered Beef and Vegetables........219
BBQ Kangaroo Meat on Hoba (Japanese Magnolia Leaves)...221
Chicken Kara-age..222
Deep-Fried Chicken Wrapped in Nori.....................................223
Grilled Chicken Wings..225
Varieties of Yakitori..227
Duck, Tataki-Style...229

Diced Pork in Broth

200 g/7 oz pork loin with skin, cut into 2.5cm cubes

1 tablespoon sake

4 tablespoons katakuri-ko (potato starch)

Vegetable oil for deep-fry

4 tablespoons soy sauce

80 ml/2½ fl oz water

2 tablespoons caster sugar

1 tablespoon grated ginger

1 clove garlic, crushed

1 tablespoon mirin

4 Mitsuba, Japanese water cress

20 g/¾ oz julienned ginger

OPTIONAL
1 tablespoon wa-garashi Japanese mustard or English mustard

NOTE – blowtorch for scorching the pork

1. With a knife, make slits over the pork.
2. Place the pork in a bowl, add sake and combine.
3. Coat the pork with katakuri-ko and set aside for 5 minutes.
4. Heat the oil in a wok or heavy-based pan to 180°C/350°F. Deep-fry the pork, then drain it well on paper towels.
5. Combine the soy sauce, water, sugar, ginger and garlic in a pan then bring to the boil over a moderate heat. Add the pork and simmer until the sauce is reduced and glossy. Before taking off the heat, add mirin and toss to mix through. Remove the pork from the heat.
6. Scorch the pork skin with blowtorch.
7. Serve pork with top with Mitsuba and ginger.

Chicken thigh fillet or lamb fillet can be substituted for pork in this recipe.

Deep-Fried Crispy Pork with Shichimi Salt

150 g/5 oz lean pork, sliced thinly. (Your butcher can do this for you.)

2 tablespoons katakuri-ko (potato starch)

Shichimi (Japanese seven spices) for serving

Freshly grounded salt for serving

Vegetable oil for deep frying

1. Place the pork slices onto a cutting board and pound with the back of the blade until very thin.
2. Coat the pork with potato starch and transfer onto a baking tray. Leave for 15 minutes.
3. Grill the pork lightly.
4. Meanwhile, prepare oil in a wok or heavy-based pan and heat up to 180°C/350°F. Deep-fry the pork until crispy, then drain it well on paper towels.
5. Serve on a plate and sprinkle with shichimi and salt.

Stir-Fried Rolled Pork with Shishitou

200 g/7 oz lean pork thinly sliced

8 shishitou, Japanese green chilli, slice half lengthways and deseed

2 tablespoons potato starch for coating

A few drops of vegetable oil

4 tablespoons teriyaki sauce (see page 227 'Yakitori')

Optional roasted white sesame seeds

16 Toothpicks

1 Place a piece of sliced of pork on a chopping board.

2 Arrange the halved shishito on the short end of pork. Roll tightly.

3 Coat with potato starch and secure with a toothpick.

4 Drop oil in a frying pan and heat up until surface seems to shimmer slightly, and then transfer the rolls to the pan. Stir-fry until cooked, occasionally shaking the pan.

5 Drizzle teriyaki sauce over the pork and sauté for a couple of minutes.

6 Serve on a plate and sprinkle with sesame seeds.

=/=/=/=/=/=/=/=/=/=/=/=/=/=/=/=/=/=

Pork Shabu-Shabu salad

200 g/7 oz pork loin, thinly sliced or sliced pork

1 tablespoon sake

1 tablespoon usukuchi-syoyu, light colour soy sauce

2 tablespoons Barbados or brown sugar

2 habanero chili, halved and deseeded, and chopped

1 teaspoon olive oil

4 lime wedges

Hydro mini salad leaves

1 Place pork in a tray and drizzle with sake. Allow to stand for two minutes.

2 Place pork into pot of boiling water and allow to blanche, remove when cooked and refresh in cold water.

3 Meanwhile, add the soy sauce and Barbados sugar in a saucepan and cook until the sugar is dissolved. Remove from the heat and include habanero chilli and olive oil, mix together.

4 Toss the blanched pork with the sauce.

5 Arrange the pork on a plate top with the salad leaves and lime wedges.

Kushi-age, Deep-Fried Skewered Beef and Vegetables

TO MAKE 6 SKEWERED KUSHI-AGE

12 cubes lean rump beef, pork or chicken

6 shishi-tou, Mild green pepper (available from Asian or Japanese grocery shops) or green capsicum, cut into bit-sized pieces

1 small onion, cut into 12 wedges (do not separate layers)

6 quail eggs, boiled and shelled off

150 g/5 oz plain flour for coating

2 eggs, beaten

About 480 g/17 oz dry breadcrumbs (Japanese breadcrumbs, if available, are slightly coarser than Western ones)

Hatcho-miso puree

1 tablespoon Hatcho-miso

1 teaspoon Mirin

1 teaspoon Caster sugar

1 tablespoon sour cream

Vegetable oil for deep frying

OTHER OPTIONAL INGREDIENTS
mushrooms (such as common mushroom, shiitake mushroom), asparagus, eggplant, pumpkin, French beans, okra or garlic.

6 bamboo skewers

1 Skewer beef, pork or chicken, shishito and a quail egg onto bamboo sticks.

2 To make Hatcho-miso puree, place miso, mirin and sugar in a small pot and cook until the sugar is dissolved. Remove from the heat and allow to slightly cool. Add sour cream and combine well.

3 Arrange flour, beaten egg and breadcrumbs in separate bowls.

4 Coat the individual skewered meats with flour, dip into beaten egg, and then place into the breadcrumbs to coat.

5 Prepare oil in a deep heavy pan and heat up the oil to 170°C/325°F.

6 Over moderate heat deep fry until golden brown and drain on kitchen paper or wire rack.

7 Serve with Hatcho-miso puree.

BBQ Kangaroo Meat on Hoba (Japanese Magnolia Leaves)

200 g/7 oz Kangaroo rump steak

Black pepper corns for seasoning

Sea salt for seasoning

1 tablespoon mirin

1 tablespoon sake

4 tablespoons hacchou miso, dark brown miso

1 tablespoon brown sugar

4 sun dried Hoba leaves, fig family of magnolia leave

1 tablespoon roasted white sesame seeds

1 Cut the kangaroo meat into 4 pieces (about 50 g/ 2 oz each).

2 Lightly season with pepper and salt.

3 Marinate the kangaroo meat with mirin, sake and miso for more than 30 minutes.

4 Place each steak on a hoba leaf then grill or oven bake. (Being careful to not overcook.)

5 Sprinkle over roasted white sesame seeds.

*Dried Hoba leaves are used as a vessel in regional Japanese cuisine, especially in Gifu prefecture. Instead of Hoba leaves, dried banana husks can be used as a substitute.

*Other options, wagyu beef or pork can be used instead of Kangaroo.

Chicken Kara-age

300 g/10½ oz chicken thigh, cut into bite sizes

1 tablespoon sake

⅔ tablespoon soy sauce

1 teaspoon fresh ginger juice

3 tablespoons potato starch

Vegetable oil for deep fry

4 lemon slices

1   Place the chicken, sake, soy sauce and ginger juice in a bowl or plastic bag and massage mixture until chicken is thoroughly coated. Set aside for 10 minutes.

2   Coat the marinated chicken with potato starch.

3   Prepare oil in a deep thick pan and heat to around 170°C/325°F.

4   Deep-fry chicken until cooked.

5   Drain oil on a wire rack or kitchen paper.

6   Serve with lemon slices.

Deep-Fried Chicken Wrapped in Nori

200 g/7 oz chicken thigh fillet, cut into pieces (about 40 g/1½ oz each)

60 ml/2 fl oz soy sauce

1 tblsp mirin

1 tblsp sugar

12 (5x5cm) square nori sheets

2 tablespoons potato starch

4 lemon wedges

Vegetable oil for deep-fry

1 Marinate the chicken with soy sauce, mirin and sugar for 30 minutes.

2 Pat the chicken dry with kitchen paper.

3 Coat the chicken with katakuri-ko (potato starch).

4 Like a parcel, wrap each chicken with a nori sheet. Allow the moisture from the chicken to bend the sheets.

5 Prepare oil in a heavy deep pan and heat it up to 180°C/350°F. Deep fry chicken until crispy or cooked.

6 Serve with lemon wedges.

Grilled Chicken Wings

8 chicken wings

1 clove garlic, grated

Freshly grounded salt

A pinch of dry shredded chilli or chilli powder

1 tablespoon macadamia nut oil or vegetable oil

4 lemon wedges

4 maple leave shaped cucumber for garnish

WASABI-DIPPING SAUCE

1 tablespoon wasabi or as your preference

2 tablespoons sour cream

1 tablespoon grated daikon radish

1 Massage the chicken wings with the garlic, salt, chili and oil in a container or zipped plastic bag. Refrigerate for more than 30 minutes.

2 To prepare wasabi-dipping sauce, combine with all ingredients together in a small bowl and set aside.

3 Drop a tablespoon of oil into a frying pan and heat. Place chicken wings and cook with a lid over on a low heat for 2 minutes. Remove the lid and stir until cooked, occasionally turning them over with tongs.

4 Serve with lemon wedges and cucumber.

5 Aside with wasabi-dipping sauce.

Varieties of Yakitori

TO MAKE 6 SKEWERED

300 g/10½ oz chicken thigh or breast fillet, cut into 12 bite-size cubes

2 thick spring onion stems, trimmed and cut into 4 cm

6 bamboo skewers

1 Prepare the sauces and set aside.

2 Skewer chicken and spring onion repeatedly onto bamboo skewers.

3 Grill or cook in a frying pan, turning often and occasionally brushing with sauce until cooked.

4 Serve on a plate.

Yakitori in Teriyaki Flavour

TERIYAKI SAUCE:

3 tablespoons soy sauce

2 teaspoons caster sugar

1 teaspoon mirin

1 Combine all the ingredients together in a small saucepan and cook over the low heat until the sauce becomes smooth texture.

Yakitori Sprinkled with Shichimi Pepper

½ teaspoon shichimi (Japanese seven spices)

A pinch of salt

1 Combine shichimi and salt in a small bowl.

Yakitori with Wasabi Miso

2 tablespoons miso

1 tablespoon caster sugar

1 teaspoon wasabi paste, add extra as your preference

1 Combine miso and caster sugar in a small pan and cook until the sugar has dissolved. Cool it down and mix with wasabi paste.

Duck, Tataki-Style

2 tablespoons sake

A pinch of salt

200 g/7 oz duck breast with skin on

60 ml/2 fl oz rice vinegar

2 tablespoons caster sugar

50 g/2 oz ginger, peeled and finely chopped

1 tablespoon chopped spring onion

1 tablespoon mirin

½ brown onion, thinly sliced rings

1 Sprinkle sake and salt over the duck.

2 Wrap the duck with a muslin cloth.

3 Prepare steamer and arrange the wrapped duck on the top of steamer.

4 Steam for 15 minutes over low heat with a lid on.

5 Meanwhile, combine rice vinegar, sugar, ginger, spring onion, mirin and onion in a small bowl.

6 Transfer duck onto the chopping board without the cloth.

7 Thinly sliced.

8 Serve the steamed duck with the sauce spooned over the top.

ACKNOWLEDGEMENTS

I'd like to start by saying thank you for the opportunity to write this new book, *Sake*. I would like to thank the Managing Director Ms Fiona Schultz and Production Director Olga Dementiev of New Holland Publishing. Fiona san thank you for your constant support over the years, and Olga san, your interest and passion towards the Japanese culture has been very refreshing.

I am always very grateful towards all my friends, old and new, that have supported me through these times. My respectable friend Jill Elias, Leigh and Jennine Colacino, Judy Crawford, Ted and Jennifer Takita, International Sake Sommelier Jin Nakamura and my amazing assistant Kanako Wada.

I would like to thank the General Manager Mr Ogawa, Mr Kojima and Mr Matsumura of JFC Sydney, and Mr Kazawa of JFC Tokyo.

Special thanks go to the 28 premium Japanese sake brewing companies that took part and made this book possible, without your history I could have never succeeded in writing this publication.

Finally, I wish to thank my wife Keiko for all her support and patience, my daughter Yuzuka and son Gotarou.

None of this would have been possible without all of your help, thank you.

Culinary regards,
Hideo Dekura

SPECIAL THANKS TO:
• Claudio's Seafood
• Ceramic Studio & Gallery En
• Harris Farm Markets
• Huon Salmon
• Japan Food Corporation Australia
• Kikkoman Australia